The Alternative Defence Commiss
up in 1981 by the Lansbury Hou
with the School of Peace Studie
members include people with a wi
Appendix C) who have in commo
nuclear disarmament in Britain.

ALTERNATIVE DEFENCE COMMISSION

Without the Bomb

Non-nuclear Defence Policies
for Britain

PALADIN
Granada Publishing

Paladin Books
Granada Publishing Ltd
8 Grafton Street, London W1X 3LA

Published by Paladin Books 1985

ISBN 0-586-08527-0

Printed and bound in Great Britain by
Collins, Glasgow

Set in Baskerville

Contents

Acknowledgements

The Alternative Defence Commission and the Lansbury House Trust Fund owe a special debt of gratitude to Howard Clark who has worked tirelessly to produce this shorter, yet also updated, version of the original report of the Commission. We are indebted to Andrew Kelly for the appendix to Chapter 2.

Our thanks also go to the Joseph Rowntree Charitable Trust, the Barrow and Geraldine S. Cadbury Trust, the Northern Dairies Education Trust, the Joyce Mertz-Gilmore Foundation, the Cheney Peace Settlement and several private donors without whose financial support the project could not have been undertaken.

I know of nothing that has occurred in our time where greater optimism must be maintained . . . than in this whole business of beginning disarmament, of relieving tension in the world. The alternative is so terrible that you can merely say this: all the risks you take in trying to advance are as nothing compared to doing nothing, to sitting on your hands.

President Eisenhower, press conference, 17 July 1957

Foreword

In April 1983 the Alternative Defence Commission published a report which *The Guardian* hailed in an editorial as 'a document of profound importance to the future of British politics'. The report broke new ground in the debate about nuclear weapons. Its starting point was that Britain should reject such weapons and refuse to have them based on its territory. What was new about it was that it made a careful and detailed examination of the alternative defence policies that a non-nuclear Britain might adopt.

The report has had a significant impact. But if the ideas it puts forward are to enter the mainstream of British politics a much wider debate will be necessary that reaches beyond specialists in the field of defence and strategic studies and those with a particular interest in peace and disarmament. There is an urgent need for a debate about non- nuclear alternatives on the scale and of the intensity of debates about other aspects of nuclear policies. This was the thinking behind the writing of this present book. It presents the main ideas of the earlier report, but without some of the more technical arguments and references. The language is clear and straightforward, yet at the same time the book manages to convey the complexities of the debate. It also takes account of the developments in NATO thinking and strategy that have occurred since the first report was written.

There is ample evidence of a deep and widespread disquiet about the nuclear strategy of Britain and NATO as a whole and a conviction that new strategies must be developed. The clearest manifestation of this has been the massive protests in recent years throughout Western Europe against the deployment of cruise and Pershing II missiles.

Side by side with this there has been a spate of books and reports, written from various perspectives but all trying to grapple with the intellectual and moral problems posed by nuclear weapons. One such was the report of the Palme Commission which promoted the notion of 'common security' and put forward a number of concrete proposals for building up East – West confidence, including the establishment of a nuclear-free corridor in Central Europe. Another was *The Church and the Bomb*, the report of the Church of England working group on which I had the privilege of working. Though the Synod (governing body) of the Church of England did not adopt the report, it went further than it had ever done before, calling for NATO to accept a no first use of nuclear weapons policy. The report was also unique among documents produced by the Church in that it rapidly became a bestseller, testifying to the immense public interest in the issue.

Even more striking, however, have been the critiques of current strategy from influential military and political figures on both sides of the Atlantic. In this country the former Chief of the Defence Staff, Field Marshal Lord Carver, has called for a no first use policy. In the United States, the former Secretary of State for Defence, Robert MacNamara – who played a major role in shaping NATO policy in the 60s – also joined with other leading public figures in calling for a no first use commitment by NATO. Taken seriously, such a commitment would require a fundamental shift in NATO doctrine and the restructuring of its forces.

President Reagan himself has clearly sensed the popular desire to move away from defence based on threats of mutual annihilation. Unfortunately his 'Star Wars' project – the plan to put laser weapons on satellites to destroy Soviet missiles as soon as they were launched – would make matters worse not better. Mr Reagan argues that such a system could make nuclear war obsolete by providing the US with a protective shield against nuclear attack. But this is a dangerous illusion. His own specialists acknowledge that at best such a system would give only very partial protection. It would provide no defence whatever against nuclear weapons on aircraft or cruise missiles and it could not destroy more than a certain proportion of the longer-range ballistic missiles against which it is aimed. The system would be hideously expensive, and undo the work of the Anti-Ballistic Missile Treaty signed in 1972. It would certainly stimulate a new arms race in space, and at the end of it all the situation would be even more dangerous than it is at present. Even today, before any of the proposed new weapons have begun to be built or tested, the Star Wars project is threatening whatever slim chance there was of success in the new round of US–Soviet negotiations on nuclear weapons at Geneva.

Compared to such fantasies, the proposals of the Commission strike a note of commonsense and reality. The Commission does not pretend to have any magic solution. There is, it acknowledges, no escaping from risks, whatever defence policy is adopted. The key concept in its approach is that of 'defensive deterrence', that is to say deterrence based not on the threat of destroying an opponent's society but on making aggression costly – in political as well as military terms. It is akin to the defence mechanisms of certain insects whose colouring warns potential predators that they will be difficult to swallow and even more difficult – perhaps even fatal – to digest.

The possibilities explored include preparations for conventional warfare with a strongly defensive emphasis similar to that adopted by Sweden, defence 'in depth' with widely dispersed forces, guerrilla warfare, or non-violent civilian resistance. In the last analysis, of course, war in any form would be an immense and terrible tragedy. The aim must always be prevention. At the same time we have to recognise that no system is foolproof and so our defence cannot be allowed to take a form which might involve global destruction in the event of war. The risks are too great. Yet even if they were not so great, if for instance we could expect by some miracle to avoid the destruction of our own society in the event of war, the crime of killing millions of human beings is one that we dare not continue to contemplate.

Of course Mr Reagan claims that the Star Wars system is also defensive; what could be more defensive than a system designed to destroy nuclear missiles in flight? But this is to treat technology in isolation from its military and political context. Clearly if one country continues to deploy nuclear weapons but at the same time starts to acquire the ability to destroy the nuclear weapons of the other side, it will be regarded by the opponent as posing a greater threat than ever before. Thus Star Wars is a 'technical fix' taken to its ultimate and absurd limit. By contrast the Commission favours a system which *in its entirety* has a clearly defensive purpose and which involves a progressive reduction in the deployment of threatening technology.

The report makes an important point when it observes that security is not solely a question of the military defences a country possesses. A country's foreign policy, and its political and economic relations with other states, also have a critical bearing on the issue. Thus the increased economic cooperation between East and West in Europe during the period of détente in the 70s means that Europe today is more interdependent that ever before, and that even a conventional war in Europe would have disastrous economic consequences for the whole of Europe. This itself is a significant disincentive to aggression which could be further strengthened, as the report suggests, if it was known in advance that the civilian population were ready to engage in mass non-cooperation in the event of an attempted takeover or occupation. Those of us who are convinced that in the nuclear age it is necessary that war itself be abolished will particularly welcome the call in the report for a serious investigation into the possibilities of non-violent dissuasion and resistance. There is, of course, no incompatibility between this and seeking to persuade governments to adopt military postures which are clearly defensive and non-provocative.

The objection is often made that in Eastern Europe people are unable to protest against the military policies of their own governments. But this is no longer entirely the case. It is true that mass public demonstrations on the streets are not permitted – except in support of government policies. But in East Germany for example the Federation of Protestant Churches has publicly recorded its rejection of 'the spirit, logic and practice of deterrence' and in accordance with this has protested against the deployment of new intermediate range missiles in the East as well as the West. The British Council of Churches enjoys a close relationship with the Protestant churches of East Germany, and we find that their experts too stress such concepts as 'defensive defence', 'unilateral initiatives', and 'common security'.

In other countries in Eastern Europe significant voices have been raised against aspects of Warsaw Pact policies. In Hungary a small but independent peace movement has arisen opposed to the deployment of nuclear weapons in Europe. In Czechoslovakia, the human rights organization, Charter 77, has called for the withdrawal of US and Soviet forces from both parts of Europe and the creation of a European nuclear free zone, and in Poland the Solidarity activist, Jacek Kuron, has made a similar call.

Moreover, even at government level there have been clear indications that East European states are keen to maintain détente in Europe and have at times exerted a positive pressure on Soviet leaders.

The fear underlying the questions about Eastern Europe is of course that the Western peace movements could weaken western defence without the possibility of parallel pressure being exerted on the governments of the Soviet Union and the Warsaw Pact countries. Clearly critics of government policies in the West do have much greater freedom of action and possibility to organize than their counterparts in the Soviet Bloc. But if the threat from NATO is visibly reduced, particularly by the renunciation of nuclear weapons, it is likely that this would generate expectations and demands from below in Eastern Europe, and from the Churches, for reciprocal steps by the Warsaw Pact, and that some Eastern European governments would also be keen to encourage reciprocation by the Soviet Union in the hope of consolidating their improved relations with the West. Moreover, the Soviet Union has itself in the past supported plans for nuclear-free zones in Europe so that there would at least be a reasonable chance of achieving the mutual withdrawal of nuclear weapons from the continent.

In any case, the Commission is not suggesting that Britain and Western Europe should abandon defence preparations altogether. Britain clearly does have legitimate defence interests. These, however, will never be met if we go on believing that nuclear weapons are simply bigger and better bombs. Because they threaten destruction on a global scale, these weapons have changed the very nature and concept of war. Einstein indeed has been proved right in his reflection that everything in our century has changed except our way of thinking.

In one sense the aims of the present book are modest; to examine with care, and without baulking at any of the difficulties, the possibilities of non-nuclear defence. Yet they are also part of a wider project involving many different individuals and bodies to take up Einstein's challenge and revolutionize modes of thought and action that have begun to threaten our very existence.

Paul Oestreicher

Introduction

'Wouldn't Britain be defenceless without nuclear weapons?' Although many people feel perturbed by the build-up of nuclear arsenals and sense that 'the balance of terror' is an increasingly dangerous and unacceptable gamble, they still see no alternative to nuclear defence. Yet most of the countries technically capable of manufacturing nuclear weapons have so far decided *not* to do so. Most countries in the world neither have nuclear weapons themselves nor are members of nuclear alliances.

Britain, moreover, is in a unique position. It is *triply* nuclear – it not only possesses its own nuclear weapons, but also belongs to an alliance whose strategy relies on nuclear weapons, and it has foreign nuclear weapons based on its soil.

The Alternative Defence Commission set out to explore unilateral nuclear disarmament as a practical as well as a principled policy. Its first report, *Defence Without the Bomb*, published in April 1983, examined the choices which would be open to Britain if it abandoned its own nuclear weapons and refused to have US nuclear weapons based on its territory.

Defence Without the Bomb thus looked at British defence from first principles – what needs to be defended, against what, and by what means? But it also examined the political and military realities of the present situation – the dangers we are in and the practical possibilities for moving away from the perilous confrontation between the military blocs in Europe.

The policy favoured in *Defence Without the Bomb* was that Britain should seek to remain in NATO *providing* that NATO could be persuaded to end its reliance on nuclear weapons. Some members of the Commission believed that a non-nuclear Britain would immediately have to withdraw from NATO but most concluded that there was a strong case for staying in on certain conditions. Not only would this have the advantage of continuing the collective defence of Western Europe, but, in view of the strength of anti-nuclear feeling in other NATO countries, it might be the most effective way of influencing NATO decisions.

If NATO did adopt a non-nuclear policy in Europe, one of its main aims would be to lower the level of confrontation between East and West. Any military policy it adopted should therefore be clearly defensive, not capable of posing a military threat to Eastern Europe but strictly confined to deterring a Soviet offensive. Non-nuclear *defensive* deterrence, as against nuclear *retaliatory* deterrence, would make the most of political factors which would inhibit Soviet aggression – such as the economic interdependence of Eastern and Western Europe, and their interests in common security.

Every defence policy involves risks; none can offer foolproof guarantees of security. However, the risks of 'defensive deterrence' are not as great as those of nuclear deterrence. By its very nature, defensive deterrence would tend to reduce tension and thus the likelihood of war being launched by mistake or of pressures towards pre-emption. And, if deterrence should fail, the war would be less destructive. At the same time, the possibilities for further negotiated arms reductions and peaceful cooperation would correspondingly be improved.

Although these considerations favour a clearly defensive strategy, NATO would still require some capacity to counterattack. This should be evidently limited: sufficient to push back invaders but not to launch an attack; and counter-attacks should be directed only against enemy forces, not against cities or the population as a whole. If war is necessary, it must at least seek to be just; it should not only be fought in a just cause but it should use means which do not violate the principles of justice and which discriminate between combatant and non-combatant.

If NATO cannot be persuaded to a non-nuclear policy for Europe, our view is that Britain should withdraw from the alliance. In this case, a non-aligned, non-nuclear Britain should aim to deter attack by making an invasion prohibitively costly.

The defence policies of Sweden and Switzerland partly serve as models for such a 'high entry price' strategy.

The Commission also considered strategies which could be used in the event of military defeat or if a war was becoming too destructive. Such 'fall-back' strategies – sabotage, popular non-cooperation and other forms of civil resistance – might be used to frustrate an occupying power.

This short book explains the Alternative Defence Commission's recommendations and aims to make the thinking behind them more accessible to a wider public. At the same time, however, events have moved on since we wrote *Defence Without the Bomb*. Tension has already increased with NATO's deployment of nuclear-armed cruise and Pershing II missiles in Europe, Soviet counter-deployments in East Germany and Czechoslovakia, and the new Soviet boast that it has submarine-based nuclear missiles within ten minutes' flight time of Washington.

There is also another development: whereas it was possible to write about NATO's conventional deployments in Europe being defensive, this policy is now changing – and in the wrong direction. NATO is adopting a more offensive conventional battle-plan for central Europe. Even though the policies of AirLand Battle and Follow-on Force Attack (Deep Strike) may not be implemented in full, it has been decided to incorporate elements of them into NATO strategy, and the new weapons and targeting systems which would be needed for a fully-fledged Deep Strike are under development. The Soviet Union, too, shows no signs of switching to a less offensive strategy. Both military blocs protest that they are defensive, yet each feels increasingly threatened and becomes more inclined to think in terms of pre-emptive responses to threats.

The most hopeful development is the increasingly searching examination of defence policy. Within NATO countries there is a growing concern to raise the nuclear threshold. Especially important, in view of West Germany's crucial place in East-West relations, is the call of its main opposition party – the Social Democratic Party (SPD) – for a basic reorientation of security policy. While the SPD sees a need for a minimal level of nuclear deterrence, it urges NATO expressly to renounce the first use of nuclear weapons, replacing battlefield nuclear missiles with an unmistakably defensive conventional deterrence. It also advocates a European nuclear weapons-free zone and a nuclear freeze.

Many voices associated with mainstream thinking within the alliance now also plead for increased reliance on conventional deterrence; and it is highly significant that people of the stature of McGeorge Bundy, George Kennan, Robert McNamara and Gerard Smith – who themselves have been closely involved with US nuclear policy – are today leading advocates of a policy of no-first-use of nuclear weapons.

Several important studies have been published since *Defence Without the Bomb* was written. The European Security Study (ESECS) and its report, *Strengthening Conventional Deterrence*, are particularly significant since they involved the participation of many senior American and European defence strategists and also because NATO observers attended their deliberations. While we welcome ESECS's willingness to consider ways of reducing NATO's reliance on nuclear weapons, we are critical of its proposals for a more offensive mode of defence. A different tendency is represented in Britain by the Just Defence group which advocates entirely defensive conventional preparations for NATO, making the most of the defensive possibilities of the new technologies.

In Britain, defence remains a major political issue. And this concern is not likely to abate. While the SDP-Liberal Alliance is divided and unclear over many defence issues, it is united on the importance of seeking some measures of arms control and military disengagement in Europe. In July 1984, the Labour Party produced the most complete rethink of its defence policy for decades, a document which was adopted as party policy at the 1984 annual conference. Labour is now explicitly committed to British unilateral nuclear disarmament, the withdrawal of US nuclear bases from Britain, and urging NATO to move to a policy of no-first-use of nuclear weapons.

Despite the similarities in approach and tone to *Defence Without the Bomb*, there are some significant differences between Labour's policy and our recommendations. The Labour Party intends to remain under the US nuclear umbrella: we believe that Britain should remain in NATO only if NATO replaces its reliance on nuclear deterrence. The Labour policy would try to encourage NATO to change in a non-nuclear direction but does not contemplate withdrawal if there is no such change in NATO's position.

There are also important differences in the range of defence options brought into view. We stress that a non-nuclear defence policy needs to take full account of its own peculiar risks – especially the possibility of nuclear blackmail. We suggest that the risk of nuclear blackmail is more remote than is often thought, but we give an important place to civil resistance as a 'fall-back' strategy in the face of military defeat or threatened nuclear escalation. Realism requires a full consideration of the risks involved in any military policy, and an effort to mitigate its worst consequences. The dangers of a defensive military policy pale – albeit not into insignificance – when seen in relation to the infinite gamble of nuclear deterrence.

The debate on non-nuclear defence for Britain and NATO is at an early stage. This shorter and less technical book has sought to take account of recent developments and so updates *Defence Without the Bomb*. Readers who wish to pursue some of these issues in more detail are referred to the original book or to the Commission's forthcoming follow-up report which will look in similar detail at the politics of alternative defence, the political options for Europe, disarmament policies, possibilities for military disengagement and steps to enhance global security.

1. Thinking about War and Defence

Conventional, chemical, biological or nuclear – modern war is a disaster. This century has seen a war fought in a just cause degenerate into the wholesale slaughter of people whose 'crime' was merely to live in the wrong country. It has seen science and technology degraded; not harnessed to the purposes of human fulfilment but pressed into military service.

Terror from the air – a tactic first used against civilians by fascist Italy and Spain in the 1930s – had by the end of the Second World War become standard military practice. Whole cities became the targets for bombs which killed soldier and civilian, adult and child alike. With the bombing raids on Coventry, Dresden and Tokyo, war reached a new depth of indiscriminate devastation. This was *total war*, where whole societies were under attack and everyone was treated as a combatant.

The First World War had been unprecedentedly destructive, claiming perhaps as many as 15 million lives, nearly half of them civilians. This toll was dwarfed in the Second World War, when between 40 and 50 million people lost their lives, with perhaps twice as many civilian deaths as military. Yet the final acts of the war – the bombing of Hiroshima and Nagasaki – gave warning of a previously unimaginable scale of destruction, of a kind of warfare that could extinguish human existence. The single bomb dropped on Hiroshima had, by November 1945, killed twice as many people as all the German bombing raids on Britain.

Forty years later, the world's nuclear arsenals are equivalent in their destructive power to 1,250,000 Hiroshima bombs – the equivalent of more than three tons of TNT per head of the world's population.

THE NUCLEAR DANGER

It has become impossible to quantify the enormities of a nuclear exchange. In addition to the lethal effects of the blast, heat and radiation, many millions of people in combatant *and* non-combatant countries would die from disease and starvation as the world's economy and agricultural production collapse. In addition, recent scientific research indicates that a large nuclear war could have a drastic impact on the world's climate. Cooling and reductions in sunlight could cause massive crop failures and general ecological catastrophe. Such a nuclear winter would threaten the survival of the remainder of the world's population.

The 'security' offered by nuclear deterrence depends on deterrence *never* failing. No rational mind would seek to bring about such a catastrophe. But, whether by accident or by miscalculation, the peril of nuclear war has never been greater.

Nuclear deterrence requires a perpetual readiness actually to use nuclear weapons; a chain of command which can be counted on unquestioningly to launch a nuclear strike, a chain of people trained to treat every exercise drill as the 'real thing'. Now the two superpowers, thus prepared, confront each other with nuclear missiles only a few minutes' flight time from each other's capital cities.

New, highly accurate warhead guidance systems could combine with dramatically improved satellite reconnaissance and submarine detection to threaten an opponent's capacity to retaliate – a capacity that is intrinsic to the concept of *mutual* nuclear deterrence. Perhaps neither side will ever achieve the goal of being able to launch a 'disarming' first strike which could almost neutralize the other's nuclear force. But if either gains the ability to track and destroy even a high proportion of the other's missile-carrying submarines and to locate and destroy missiles in their silos, then there would be strong pressure in an acute crisis to strike first. This might arise from the temptation to seize a significant military advantage, the delusion that it is possible for one side to 'win' a nuclear war, or out of fear of a pre-emptive strike from the other side. The superpowers are poised at a point where, for their nuclear deterrents to be 'credible', they may feel compelled to move towards a policy of 'launch on warning' – that is, of automatic retaliation as soon as the alarm is sounded. When there is so little time for checking information, a computer malfunction or operator error could trigger a nuclear war.

In 1980–81, US computers mistakenly indicated a Soviet attack about 150 times. On four of these occasions, US strategic forces were alerted, while in one incident it took six minutes to establish that a warning of a Soviet nuclear submarine attack was an error.

Human miscalculation cannot be ruled out either, whether through the kind of brinkmanship exhibited during the Cuban missile crisis in 1962 or a sudden, more local flare-up. The shooting down of the Korean airliner by the Soviet Union in 1983 and the sinking of the *General Belgrano* by Britain in 1982 do not inspire confidence in the crisis management processes of at least two of the nuclear powers. According to British government statements, not only did the war cabinet order the attack on the *Belgrano* in ignorance of the ship's change of course, but at the very time it did so, peace negotiations were under way in Washington. The most favourable interpretation of this event is that the right hand did not know what the left hand was doing.

As things stand, any war between the superpowers is almost bound to go nuclear. At the strategic level, their arsenals are on a hair trigger. At the level of the battlefield, both sides have integrated short-range nuclear weapons into their conventional forces. NATO policy is to seek to counter a Soviet conventional attack at first with its own conventional forces, escalating to short-range battlefield nuclear weapons if it is losing. However, these weapons are based so near the front line that they could quickly be threatened with direct capture. Commanders, amid all the confusion of battle, would face the choice of 'use 'em or lose 'em'.

Once the nuclear threshold is crossed, the pressure towards escalation will be virtually uncontrollable – from 'battlefield' nuclear weapons up to 'intermediate-range' missiles aimed at targets inside the Soviet Union and on to all-out nuclear war. It is utter folly to put one's trust in the possibility of keeping a nuclear war limited when intelligence about the developing battle is likely

3

to have vital gaps, when complex and momentous decisions have to be made almost instantly under conditions of enormous psychological stress and when command, communication, control and information systems are highly vulnerable to accidental disruption or deliberate paralysis through a decapitation strike.

The 'balance of terror' has always been precarious; its stability is now being further undermined by strategic and technological developments which hugely increase the pressure towards pre-emption in a crisis.

The greatest source of military danger to Britain is the present high level of military confrontation between the blocs. As well as suffering the traumas of a nuclear winter, in a nuclear war between the superpowers, Britain would also be a direct target, both because of its own nuclear forces and because of the presence of a host of US bases and facilities. In fact, US nuclear bases could put Britain in the front line of a nuclear war even when the British government actually disagreed with US policy in a particular crisis. Already, US forces in Britain have been put on nuclear alert without prior consultation with the British government, and arrangements for consultation remain vague.

Britain would also be a target in its own right as nuclear weapons are integrated into its fighting forces from the Polaris submarines through several hundred nuclear-capable aircraft right down to nuclear depth-charges and artillery shells.

There are no justifications for the possession of nuclear weapons by Britain which do not apply to other countries. British governments admit no doubts that the US is totally committed to defend Europe. Yet, officially, the principal rationale for the British nuclear force is that European NATO needs nuclear weapons in its own hands, in addition to relying on the US guarantee to use nuclear weapons in defence of Europe. If Taiwan or South Korea (and increasing numbers of smaller states) followed this logic, they too would want their own nuclear force. It should be recognized that possession of nuclear weapons by one non-superpower is an incentive to proliferation by others.

In pursuing their nuclear policies, British governments have incurred substantial and rapidly increasing costs, while the determination to retain British nuclear weapons actually serves as an obstacle to negotiations for multilateral nuclear disarmament. Even though Britain's nuclear weapons are assigned to NATO and rely on US targeting information, the government has refused to allow them to be included in arms negotiations: the British nuclear force was therefore not considered in either the Strategic Arms Reduction Talks (START) or the Intermediate Nuclear Force (INF) negotiations. On the other hand, Neil Kinnock's talks with the Soviet leader Konstantin Chernenko indicate that if Britain unilaterally renounced its nuclear weapons, the Soviet Union would recognize that it was in its interests to offer some significant reciprocation.

In a world containing thousands of nuclear weapons, there can be no foolproof policy for avoiding nuclear war. On balance, removing nuclear weapons from British soil would in our view reduce the risk of an all-out nuclear attack on Britain. But our main reason for urging this policy is as an independent step to make nuclear war itself less likely. British nuclear disarmament should be part of a broader initiative, aiming to secure the removal of tactical nuclear weapons from Europe – East and West – and, if possible, the establishment of a nuclear weapons-free zone covering the whole of Europe.

MORALITY AND WAR

War always raises urgent moral issues and these are posed in an especially acute form with weapons of mass destruction. Pacifists believe that war is always inherently evil. However, the dominant Western tradition for addressing these issues is that of the 'Just War'. This includes three main criteria: (a) the cause of the war must be just and also sufficiently serious; (b) the war should discriminate between combatant and non-combatant, avoiding attacks on civilians; and (c) the force used should be in proportion to the issue at stake. And where civilian casualties are unavoidable in the course of an attack upon a legitimate military target, there must be some reasonable proportion between this legitimate aim and the probable extent of civilian casualties.

Thus, in the Second World War where the cause – the defeat of Nazism and fascism – was undoubtedly just, there were testing moral problems arising from the conduct of war, in particular the strategic bombing of cities.

In practice, waging a nuclear war would massively violate the principles of discrimination and proportionality, but some people argue that there is a moral distinction between *threatening* to use nuclear weapons in order to deter nuclear attack and actually using them. This, however, presupposes that nuclear deterrence is a bluff. But the nuclear powers have to be in a constant state of readiness for war. Only with such real – physical and psychological – readiness for nuclear war can the deterrent be effective. From the crews trained to use nuclear weapons with unhesitating obedience to the military planners, there has to be absolute conviction that this threat is indeed meant. They are conscious that nuclear deterrence involves not only the risk of an eventual holocaust but a willingness to participate in unleashing it. The electors, on whose behalf they fulfil these roles, thus become a party to the process of preparing for nuclear war. Only perfect certainty that the threat of nuclear war will prevent its outbreak – a degree of certainty never possible in the complex world of international relations – could begin to excuse preparations for such an enormity.

It is important to bear in mind that nuclear deterrence is not confined to preventing *nuclear* war: NATO also threatens to use nuclear weapons if this is necessary to halt a Soviet *conventional* attack. The crux of the moral debate, then, is whether the political objective of preventing a possible Soviet occupation would justify waging a nuclear war. The answer from common sense, from the guidelines of 'Just War' theory, and from the whole ethical tradition of which it is a part, is that it would not.

Naturally, if one rejects nuclear weapons on moral grounds, one cannot ask another country to threaten or actually to wage nuclear war on one's behalf, nor grant it facilities to do so. This has important implications for Britain's relations with NATO, if a moral rejection of nuclear deterrence leads Britain to adopt a policy of unilateral nuclear disarmament.

The 'Just War' theory's concern with universally binding limits sets it firmly against the trend of warfare in the twentieth century towards ever greater and less discriminating destruction.

6

Its guidelines also suggest that in shaping a non-nuclear defence, one should reject the kind of deterrence – *retaliatory* deterrence – which threatens destruction of the opponent's society in the event of war. Instead, one should seek to devise forms of *defensive* deterrence which would not be seen as threatening and which would be clearly directed against the military forces used in the attack. The emphasis would be on bringing discrimination and proportion back into defence, minimizing the suffering of non-combatants if war does break out.

Framing a Defensive Non-nuclear Policy

The security of Europe requires reducing the levels of military confrontation. Political settlements provide a surer foundation for peace than any military threats. A defensive policy should be part of a foreign policy which seeks political agreements, especially in the areas of disarmament and tension reduction, and tries to foster social, cultural and economic contact. Often economic interdependence is as likely to restrain aggression as military factors – trade is usually a better means of gaining access to resources than conquest.

Defence should discourage aggression without threatening a potential attacker. A major build-up of offensive forces is likely to appear threatening and can actually provoke attack; it is almost certain to lead to a counter-build-up on the other side and so to an arms race. A defensive policy should aim to be non-provocative.

A defender does not need to match an aggressor's military force. In conventional warfare, the defence has certain inherent advantages – a better knowledge of the terrain and the way the society operates, shorter supply lines, prepared positions and better possibilities for mobilization. Military thinkers often assume that something like a three-to-one numerical (or some equivalent) advantage is needed by the side taking the offensive in war. As a defensive strategy requires merely that one's forces are strong enough to frustrate an attack, they do not need to be as numerous or powerful. This consideration might ease the way towards reversing the arms race by allowing a switch of focus away from the fixation on a strict numerical balance of forces.

Stability rather than exact symmetry of forces should be the goal.

A defensive strategy should aim to restrict the force an aggressor can apply. On the nuclear level, a defender can thus minimize the military temptations to a nuclear-armed state by creating few military targets that would warrant a nuclear attack. However, it is upon *political* restraints that the avoidance of nuclear war depends most critically. Neither superpower has wanted, or would in future lightly risk, the scandal and outrage, and the consequent loss of moral and political authority, that would result from using nuclear weapons against a non-nuclear opponent. Reinforcing these inhibitions is of paramount importance in preventing the use of nuclear weapons.

There can be a political component in defence. This is the battle for minds and hearts, both to challenge the aggressor's troops and population, and, addressing uncommitted opinion in the world as a whole, to win the support of third parties (the populations and governments of other countries).

Excessive military expenditure may undermine both the economy and the social stability of a country and of the whole international environment. The vast diversion of resources to military purposes worldwide serves to prevent the solution of some of the world's most pressing problems. Domestically, too, the military absorbs a large proportion of public spending and distorts scientific research and development. Even if it cannot be achieved immediately, the continuing goal must be to reduce defence expenditure on all sides.

Defence policies should not corrupt the society's declared values. Some 'democratic' countries make key decisions about defence in secret and curtail basic civil rights – Britain is a prime example. From the 1947 authorization of the manufacture of nuclear weapons to the 1970s' Polaris Improvement Programme 'Chevaline', defence decision-making has been hidden from Parliament, while the Official Secrets Act has been used to deny information less to an outside enemy than to the people of Britain itself. The banning of trade unions at GCHQ, Cheltenham, is a further example of conflict between the so-called requirements of defence and democratic rights. Some 'free' countries imprison conscientious objectors; some 'civilized' countries use torture. The very possession of nuclear weapons violates the proclaimed values of all the nuclear powers. Defence cannot be concerned only with protecting lives and territory; principles and values require no less vigilance in their defence. Indeed, there are real and vital ways in which the defence of values can continue even under enemy occupation.

BRITISH DEFENCE INTERESTS

Since the Second World War, Britain has pursued a policy of collective security in alliance with the US and the European members of NATO. For most of this time, British policy has been organized round possession of nuclear weapons and, in general, the defence of Britain has been envisaged as beginning along the east-west German border. With the loss of empire and Britain's greater involvement with Europe, the emphasis increasingly shifted from independent global commitments to shared responsibilities within the NATO alliance.

Britain has an evident interest in the security of Europe as a whole as well as in directly defending its own national boundaries and inhabitants. This security is currently threatened by the confrontation between the military blocs. In Chapter 2, we consider possible threats towards a nuclear-disarmed Britain. We discuss Britain's relationship with NATO in Chapter 3 and military defence options for Western Europe in Chapter 4.

Currently British forces still have some commitments overseas outside NATO. As our focus is the avoidance of nuclear war, we do not discuss the army's role in Northern Ireland, nor in 'aiding the civil power' in times of domestic upheaval. In the light of the change in direction of British policy since the Falklands conflict, it is vital, however, to consider the issues relating to British military intervention outside Europe.

Until the Falklands conflict, Britain's ability to wage war at a long range was in decline. At that time, with the exception of the US, no other country could have mounted a naval operation on the scale of the Task Force and, had John Nott's efforts to 'streamline' the navy come to fruition, Britain, too, would no longer have had this capacity. In view of the costs involved, we consider that Nott was realistic in doubling the extent to which

9

Britain could hope to continue to defend territories many thousands of miles from its shores. Instead, Britain should negotiate political settlements which take account of its diminishing political reach as well as of the rights of the inhabitants, as it has been ready to do over Hong Kong.

A further aspect of overseas intervention is the defence of British economic interests. As a densely populated island heavily dependent on trade, Britain could be vulnerable to economic threats. In a supplementary paper to *Defence Without the Bomb*, we discuss non-military precautions to safeguard Britain's economy against disruption of supplies.[1] But while Britain would be right to resist an economic blockade, overseas military interventions would be a disproportionate burden on its resources as well as being prohibitively risky. Rather than look to military means to protect overseas investments or to defend access to raw materials, Britain should make the most of skilled economic and diplomatic negotiation. A British or NATO Rapid Deployment Force would especially tend to exacerbate international problems; it would be much more appropriate for Britain to renew its support for the UN and other genuinely international institutions.

THE POSSIBILITY OF NUCLEAR BLACKMAIL

The gravest threat a non-nuclear power has to reckon with is nuclear blackmail or the nuclear escalation of a conventional war.

It is hard to imagine a nuclear power threatening to use nuclear weapons against a non-nuclear country unless they were already at war. Indeed, the history of the last forty years shows that even in war this threat is unlikely: it would be very difficult for any state to justify to its own people, let alone the rest of the world, a nuclear attack on a country which was not offering a nuclear threat. The circumstances in which Hiroshima and Nagasaki were bombed can hardly be repeated: now that the world knows the effects of nuclear weapons, there is a unique and widespread revulsion against the use of these weapons. Thus, the US did not use nuclear weapons either in Korea or Vietnam (though their use was contemplated); nor has the Soviet Union used them in Afghanistan.

There is a quite common idea that, outside of war, a nuclear-disarmed Britain would be threatened: 'Unless you do such and such, we will bomb you.' This would rebound disastrously on the blackmailer. Not least, it would lay waste to any hopes they may have of stemming the spread of nuclear weapons. One could assume that not only would there be strong public pressure for Britain to rearm but that other countries – countries technically capable of making nuclear weapons but so far refraining – would then decide to exercise the nuclear option.

Nevertheless, in confronting a nuclear adversary, the possibility of nuclear blackmail – or an unannounced nuclear escalation – cannot be ruled out entirely.

A non-nuclear Britain must make every effort to strengthen the political inhibitions on the use of weapons of mass destruction – chemical and biological as well as nuclear weapons. This would involve seeking public declarations from the nuclear powers that they would not use nuclear weapons against Britain and other non-nuclear countries. For its part, Britain should invite inspection in order to confirm to the Soviet Union in particular that nuclear weapons had been removed; it should also avoid the use of missiles – such as cruise missiles – which can be fitted with conventional explosives but which are especially associated with nuclear warheads.

Militarily, a non-nuclear defence strategy should seek both to minimize any offensive threat it might seem to include and to limit the military value to the opponent of weapons of mass destruction. This points to a recognizably defensive emphasis – with minimal counter-attacking capacities – and to the decentralization of command and control structures as well as a dispersed deployment of forces, avoiding large concentrations of troops and tanks.

Ultimately, a superpower could force a non-nuclear state to capitulate by using or threatening to use weapons of mass destruction. The non-nuclear state would then have to submit to occupation or to the imposition of a client regime. The defeat of the state, however, need not mean the country's essential surrender: popular resistance could still deny an occupying force 'the fruits of victory'. Either guerrilla warfare or civil resistance could serve as a 'fall-back' strategy, preventing the occupying power from establishing effective political and economic control. Such forms of resistance could keep alive the spirit of freedom and justice and prepare the ground for an eventual political liberation. These anti-occupation strategies are therefore discussed in Chapter 6.

There is one temptation that a nuclear-disarmed state should firmly resist, namely to gamble that, while both superpowers have nuclear weapons, neither will dare to use them. A country which rejects nuclear weapons on principle cannot want such weapons used on its behalf. Besides, even where a nuclear state declares that it would use nuclear weapons in defence of another, this has long been recognized as problematic: who knows how nuclear decision-makers would behave in such an extreme emergency?

Conclusions

No defence policy is free of risks. There is no ideal way to guarantee security. In advocating non-nuclear defence, we are well aware of the problems involved. However, these problems have to be weighed against the appalling and all-encompassing dangers of nuclear defence. While a policy of nuclear deterrence risks absolute catastrophe, the risks in unconditionally renouncing nuclear weapons are relatively more limited. At worst, one would be more vulnerable to invasion, occupation and subjugation, but at least life would continue and with it the chance to resist by other means.

It is not only risks which have to be weighed, but also opportunities. The nuclear arms race has reached the point where a political crisis or computer error could precipitate the world into a nuclear holocaust. In adopting a non-provocative defence policy which, rather than threaten a potential opponent, concentrated strictly on deterring attack, Britain would begin the defusing of the nuclear time-bomb in Europe. A major step would have been taken in the direction of reducing tension and the level of military confrontation. Free of its addiction to nuclear weapons, Britain would then be able to play a more constructive role in promoting disarmament and more peaceful relations in the world.

2. What Would a Non-nuclear Britain Have to Fear from the Superpowers?

In Chapter 1, we identified Britain's defence interests and discussed guidelines for a non-nuclear defence strategy. Before moving on to a detailed examination of defence options, we also need to assess what threats Britain must guard against.

Since the Falklands conflict, the British government has laid more emphasis on defending British interests in all areas of the world, as distinct from its NATO commitments. This attempt to reverse the trend of history seems short-sighted and likely to strain Britain's defence budget to breaking point. Therefore this chapter does not analyse possible contingencies in far-flung corners of the globe but concentrates solely on examining what Britain has to fear from the superpowers.

The Soviet Union has, since the Second World War, been seen as 'the enemy' against which British defence policy has mainly been directed. The US, on the other hand, has been the 'champion of the Free World', with Britain often a mere second in its corner. This 'special relationship' could be jeopardized by Britain's rejection of nuclear weapons, and in particular by Britain's refusal to house US nuclear bases; indeed, Britain could become subject to intense American resentments.

THE SOVIET THREAT

The case for a non-nuclear defence is based on a moral, political and strategic rejection of nuclear policies, not on a rosy view of the Soviet Union. A country does not grow to be a superpower unless it has military ambitions. Nevertheless, the main priority of Soviet foreign and defence policy – like any other state – is simply its own security. In particular, as 20 million Soviet citizens were killed in the Second World War, it wants to make sure that a further war is not fought on Soviet territory. From this arises its second priority: to maintain Eastern Europe as a buffer zone. This does not wholly explain the ideological control it extends to Eastern Europe and still less does it excuse the repressive character of the regimes it supports or has installed. However, it is clear that the Soviet Union is more concerned about keeping control of this buffer zone than about expansion into Western Europe.

The third goal of Soviet defence policy is to be seen as the equal of the United States. Since Khrushchev had to back down from his attempt to base nuclear missiles in Cuba in 1962, the Soviet Union has been determined to establish nuclear 'parity' with the United States – and at the Strategic Arms Limitations Talks (SALT) in the early 1970s, it was recognized that there was now 'rough parity' at the strategic nuclear level. The pursuit of parity obviously contributes to the escalation of the nuclear arms race. For instance, if NATO's deployment of cruise and Pershing II was destabilizing, the Soviet 'counter-measures' – i.e. deploying new nuclear missiles in East Germany and Czechoslovakia and announcing that it now has submarine-based nuclear missiles only a few minutes' flight time from Washington – do nothing to help restore stability. Both sides remain hooked on the idea of 'negotiating from strength'.

Some people think that the Soviet system has an inevitable drive towards world domination. However, there is much evidence that, far from seeking to 'export the revolution' at every opportunity, Soviet leaders are inclined to be pragmatic and cautious. The Soviet Union's involvement in Afghanistan, for instance, is not part of a global masterplan to establish world communism. Rather, it is typical of the tendency of the super-powers to view their neighbours as their own 'backyard'. The Soviet Union's main concern was that a friendly government was in danger. At a time when Iran was already in turmoil, and mindful that Afghanistan borders on Muslim areas of the Soviet Union, the Soviet leaders were anxious to avoid further unrest. They now find themselves embroiled in a protracted war which shows no sign of ending.

Ideology still figures prominently in the Soviet view of the world and ideological factors play some part in Soviet decision-making. In general, however, Soviet foreign policy distinguishes between preserving the interests of the Soviet state and promoting revolution elsewhere, and the interests of the Soviet Union come first. Thus, recent Third World revolutions have not been Soviet-inspired – rather, the Soviet Union has tended to become more involved once a movement is successful. The use of Soviet and Cuban troops in Africa, for instance, has been to defend newly established regimes, not to foment revolution.

Similarly, Soviet commitment to local communist parties has been strictly limited – for instance, in the 1950s supporting Nasser and Nehru at the expense of the Egyptian and Indian communist parties. During the Algerian War of Independence, rather than risk harming relations with de Gaulle, the Soviet Union gave very little help to the independence movement. More recently, from 1979 onwards, Soviet aid enabled the conservative government of North Yemen to crush the left-wing guerrilla movement, the National Democratic Front, even though the NDF was pro-Soviet in its international views and supported by neighbouring South Yemen, a close ally of the Soviet Union. While the Soviet Union has taken a strong stand on Chile since the junta's overthrow of Allende, throughout the 1970s it remained friendly with the equally dictatorial and repressive regime in Argentina because Argentina is a major grain supplier.

If ideology thus does not determine Soviet policy, it has even less influence over defence policy. Instead, three key strategic ideas have emerged out of practical considerations since the Second World War. The first is 'preparedness'. During Khrushchev's rule, one of his main criticisms of Stalin was that he had left the Soviet Union unprepared for the Nazi invasion. As a result the Soviet Union feels that it now has to be prepared for any conceivable contingency, and so it tends to overinsure.

The second strategic idea is 'forward deployment'. In the past, the Russians defeated Napoleon and Hitler through waging a war of attrition, taking advantage of the fierce winters and their huge territorial land-mass. In future, however, both in Europe and in Asia, the Soviet leadership is determined to defeat an enemy *before* they enter its territory. Accordingly, the Soviet battle-plan is therefore to carry the war, once it has started, into their opponents' territory – like a football team trained to assume that the best place to defend is in the opponents' half of the field.

The high force levels implicit in the Soviet notion of being prepared, together with the posture of forward deployment, naturally alarm the West. They could give the Soviet Union the capability to launch a surprise attack into West Germany, and this inevitably increases tension. To many Western military analysts, what the Soviet Union is capable of doing is more important than what it may at present *intend* to do. Consequently, what Soviet leaders see as precautions in defence of their own territory, the West perceives with anxiety as a threat to itself.

It does not help, of course, that each side tends to exaggerate the military power of the other. Warsaw Pact conventional forces do outnumber NATO's but they could not be confident of routing NATO's considerable conventional forces (see Appendix A).

When assessing Soviet military capability, other factors have to be considered, such as what roles these forces are expected to play and how well equipped and trained they are. As the invasions of Hungary and Czechoslovakia showed, Warsaw Pact forces are required to suppress revolt within the Eastern bloc. In addition to its involvement in Afghanistan, the Soviet Union also faces a powerful and hostile neighbour along the 4,300-mile border with China. Warsaw Pact conventional forces are in general less well trained than NATO's and, although their command structure may be better coordinated, many of the soldiers are conscripts who consider themselves as coming from subject nations. In general, they are equipped with older, sometimes near-obsolete technology.

The third development in Soviet strategic posture is the growth of its naval power. Until the Second World War, the Soviet navy was basically confined to coastal defence. Later, under both Stalin and Khrushchev, there was a large merchant marine building programme which, in turn, forced the development of a naval military capacity to defend the civilian marine. Militarily, the naval threat to the Soviet Union was also seen to change from amphibious landings to long-range nuclear attack by submarine-launched missiles and of bomber attacks from aircraft carriers. To counter this, in the early 1960s, the Soviet Union mounted its own programme of naval building. This naval expansion also has to be seen in the light of the worldwide presence of the US navy and the Soviet determination to be acknowledged as a great power of similar status.

Future policy cannot be confidently predicted; it depends on both international and domestic developments. The Soviet system is inherently secretive; Party rule is centralized and dictatorial; there are no formal channels for organized opposition or popular pressure. These characteristics may strengthen a tendency to ruthless action and military solutions, though the Soviet Union also has a powerful interest in stability.

Since it agreed to US participation in the European Security Conference at Helsinki in 1976, the USSR has recognized that the US has a legitimate role to play in Europe. Facing severe economic problems already, the Soviet leadership is aware that high arms spending harms the economy. Also, being the only place in the world surrounded by hostile communist countries, it has little reason to exacerbate its problems within the Soviet Union and Eastern Europe by occupying part of Western Europe. On the contrary, now that its fears of West Germany have been quietened and it encourages trade with the EEC, it may have growing political and economic incentives to relax its grip on Eastern Europe. The possibility of negotiating forms of disengagement and demilitarization in central Europe may therefore be greater than in the past.

Western European defence policy, however, should not depend on an optimistic assessment of the Soviet Union. If the military costs of an attack seem low, the lust for power latent in all mighty states could overrule prudent calculations, tempting Soviet leaders to overlook long-term costs in order to make short-term gains or increase their personal prestige. Some form of credible non-nuclear defence, pending moves towards effective disarmament in Europe, would clearly remain essential. One possible danger is that Eastern European unrest might spill over, especially if the West tried to intervene.

The threat of Soviet military action to include Britain in its sphere of influence, or to impose Soviet-style communism here, is very remote. The most likely military threat the Soviet Union might pose to a non-nuclear Britain which had left NATO would be in pursuit of strategic gains; for instance, in a war or at a time of crisis, it may try to seize ports – either for its own use or to deny the US use of them.

The other danger that some people fear is that a non-nuclear Britain, or Western Europe, might have to make concessions to the Soviet Union either in foreign or domestic policy. Short of direct military intervention, the Soviet Union is, however, in a weak position to put pressure on countries so far afield. And, economically, it needs trade with the West far more than the West needs trade with the Soviet Union. Indeed, the US has rather more means of influence available to it.

US Pressure

In shifting to a non-nuclear defence policy, new threats may arise. We have already discussed the possibility of military weakness tempting the Soviet Union to attack. A more startling possibility would be that the US, currently Britain's ally, should become a threat. Yet this might happen if the US sought to hold on to its nuclear bases and to obstruct the development of non-nuclear policies.

British nuclear disarmament, together with removing US nuclear bases from Britain, might arouse fears in the US that Britain was changing from being its loyal ally to becoming a potential enemy. The dangers of US hostility would be increased if a left-wing government also declared Britain non-aligned and left NATO. During the period of transition to a non-nuclear defence, intense US pressure is very likely. In the longer term, the US may still exert pressure to recover use of strategic facilities, though open use of military force is likely only in the event of a European war, when the US might seize territory from a non-aligned Britain in order to pre-empt the Soviet Union.

Britain's scrapping of its own nuclear weapons would not cause its allies great consternation – indeed, some would welcome this.

The US, however, would take a much more serious view of having to remove its nuclear weapons from Britain. In 1984, there were 135 bases and facilities planned or installed in Britain, with another thirty expected. Over 27,000 US troops are stationed here. Some bases would clearly be unacceptable to a nuclear-disarmed Britain, whatever its relationship to NATO: the Poseidon base at Holy Loch, the F-111 bases in the Midlands and East Anglia, the nuclear weapons stores.

This would be the greatest upheaval in NATO's history. In the past, France and Greece have withdrawn from NATO and in 1969 Canada refused to let nuclear weapons be based on its territory and reduced its European troop commitment from 10,000 to 3,000. At the moment, Denmark is refusing to pay its full contribution towards the siting of cruise and Pershing II missiles in Europe, while the Netherlands has delayed deployment and laid down certain conditions. But none of these has represented a fundamental challenge to NATO's nuclear strategy.

In 1966, after several years of dissent, France withdrew from NATO's military command. However, some military involvement continues through early-warning systems and in NATO exercises. It remains a member of the North Atlantic Council (NATO's political counterpart), pays regularly towards NATO's civilian costs, and has a say in appointing the NATO secretary-general. As the NATO headquarters at the time was based in France and 26,000 US soldiers were also stationed there, this partial withdrawal was disruptive. But, apart from paying for the relocation of four US bases, France has not been penalized.

Greece withdrew from the NATO military command in 1974 in protest against the Turkish invasion of Cyprus, but US bases were never expelled and Greece rejoined NATO in 1981. Currently the Greek government is actively seeking a Balkans nuclear-free zone and officially desires the removal of all US bases. In this, however, it is treading very carefully, partly so as not to offer Turkey – its bitter rival as well as fellow-member of NATO – the chance of any military advantage and partly because it depends heavily on the US for its supplies of arms.

If Britain either decided to opt for non-alignment or withdrew from NATO after failing to win it over to a non-nuclear strategy, this would be an especially damaging blow to NATO. While it is unlikely that the US would try by force to retain its bases in Britain, it could exert diplomatic and economic pressure, and could be expected to give support and encouragement to those groups within Britain opposed to the non-nuclear policies of the government. The CIA has funded and does fund organizations in Britain and at the very least a non-nuclear government should expect a vigorous and well-funded propaganda campaign against its policies.

As well as propaganda, 'covert operations' cannot be ruled out in the transition period if the US perceived the British government as being anti-American. There is little point at this stage in speculating on the possibilities of conspiracies between disgruntled British military officers or other groups and the CIA: whatever the likelihood of this being attempted, Britain is very different from countries like Chile or Guatemala and a military takeover here would be much more difficult to organize and sustain.

No doubt the US government could bring economic pressure to bear on Britain but, unless it could persuade the rest of Western Europe to join with it in applying economic sanctions, it would probably not be able to cripple the British economy. The US is less well placed than at certain periods in the past to apply pressure of this kind.

It is vital for Britain to try to act in concert with other European countries, both to maximize the effectiveness of British nuclear disarmament and as a safeguard against reprisals. At the same time, whether inside or outside NATO, British government policy should be firm and unwavering – patiently explaining changes in policy and questioning the perceptions behind current NATO strategy, while at the same time insisting on its rejection of nuclear weapons. This would need to be backed by a population prepared, in the majority, to support the new policies and if necessary to resist by mass non-cooperation any illicit attempt to seize power or thwart the democratic process.

CONCLUSION

In our view, the main threats to British security would be:

(a) involvement in a nuclear war between the great powers;

(b) involvement in a conventional war in Europe – either directly through membership of NATO or a European alliance, or as a possible strategic target if Britain was non-aligned; and

(c) that US pressure, falling short of direct military attack, might be exerted to ensure use of strategic facilities in time of peace.

3. Britain, NATO and Europe

NATO was established in 1949 as a way of guaranteeing US involvement in the defence of Western Europe and of enshrining the principle of the collective defence of Western Europe in the face of what was seen as an aggressive Soviet state. Although Europeans, especially the British, played a part in setting up NATO, the US has tended to dominate NATO policy.

Historically, NATO policy in central Europe has been defensive at the conventional level, keeping forces below the level necessary to mount an offensive into Warsaw Pact territory but sufficient to deter a Soviet conventional attack. Consistently underlying NATO conventional strategy, however, has been a willingness to use nuclear weapons to compensate for conventional weakness. In a war, NATO would quickly have to go nuclear.

Reliance on nuclear weapons is therefore fundamental to NATO thinking. NATO is a nuclear alliance. Not only do individual members – the US and Britain – have nuclear weapons, but since 1955 most *alliance* forces have been equipped with US nuclear weapons under multinational control. NATO is also committed to a policy of being willing to use nuclear weapons first: under the strategy of 'flexible response', formally adopted in 1967, NATO would use nuclear weapons if necessary to halt a Soviet *conventional* offensive.

Whether or not to remain in NATO is the most important question for Britain without the Bomb. In Britain, supporters of nuclear disarmament are divided over this crucial issue.

If British unilateralism were based only on anxiety about British safety, Britain might consider following the example of Norway and Canada – members of NATO which have publicly refused to allow nuclear weapons on their territory in peacetime.

But even this policy would not ensure safety from nuclear attack: if there is a nuclear war, there are likely to be direct strikes against both Norway and Canada, and no country will be immune from the consequences of a nuclear war. As we explained in Chapter 1, however, our view is that Britain should reject nuclear weapons on more fundamental grounds and should seek to reduce the risk of nuclear war happening at all by promoting international disarmament. In the light of this, it would be inconsistent to remain in an alliance whose strategy relied on nuclear weapons and which was, moreover, willing to use those weapons first.

A non-nuclear Britain would then have the basic choice *either* to remain a member of NATO and seek to shift it towards a non-nuclear policy, *or* to leave NATO and either be non-aligned or seek the formation of a non-nuclear European defence association independent of the US.

The most likely course is that Britain would stay in NATO. Indeed, this is central to the Labour Party's non-nuclear policy. But Labour's *Defence and Security for Britain* does not consider what would happen if NATO could not be shifted from its reliance on nuclear weapons. Our view is that Britain remaining in NATO should be explicitly conditional upon NATO's becoming a non-nuclear alliance. Thus, if NATO cannot be changed in this way, Britain would have to consider the options open if it left NATO.

Non-nuclear in NATO

1. *Conditions for Membership*
If British membership of NATO were conditional upon steps to end the alliance's reliance on nuclear weapons, Britain would have a coherent and constructive policy on NATO. There are four main steps Britain should propose towards ending NATO's reliance on nuclear weapons.

(a) *A policy of no-first-use of nuclear weapons*. This would signal NATO's intention to raise the nuclear threshold, ending its present willingness to resort to nuclear weapons against a conventional attack. If accompanied by appropriate practical measures, this would increase the credibility of NATO's defences and reduce pressure on the Soviet Union to use nuclear weapons pre-emptively. And, as the Soviet Union has made a declaration of no-first-use and invited the West to reciprocate, a mutual pledge might ease the way to further, more specific agreements.

(b) *A phased but total withdrawal of all battlefield nuclear weapons*. In order to give credibility to a no-first-use pledge, NATO would have publicly to reassess its conventional military strategy, which is at present tied to early nuclear escalation. Battlefield nuclear weapons are essentially war-fighting weapons: they tend to 'lower the threshold' between nuclear and conventional weapons as they would be deployed early in a war and against Soviet conventional forces. While Britain should urge the unilateral withdrawal of these weapons upon NATO, NATO should aim to get the greatest moral and political leverage from this withdrawal, and strongly press the Soviet Union to reciprocate. If both Soviet and NATO battlefield nuclear weapons were withdrawn, such a development would be both militarily and politically a major gain for East-West relations.

(c) *Removal of all NATO 'theatre' nuclear weapons*. NATO has an array of 'theatre' nuclear weapons, including land-based and sea-based missiles and nuclear bombers allocated to the European theatre. Removal of cruise and Pershing II is a matter of special urgency, not only because of the strategic escalation they represent as highly accurate war-fighting weapons and prime targets for a pre-emptive nuclear strike, but also because of the symbolic importance they have acquired. Removal of all 'theatre' weapons from Western Europe is a far-reaching but essential goal. It would be a further dramatic step away from the present confrontation. Priority should be given to removing land-based weapons, since these have a visible and clear-cut theatre role in NATO strategy. However, to make Western Europe a genuinely nuclear-free zone, European countries would also have to withdraw base facilities from US ships carrying nuclear weapons. And since sea-based nuclear weapons may be seen as part of the general US deterrent force and not simply as weapons assigned to the European theatre, this last step would directly raise the issue of whether or not European NATO countries should explicitly decouple their strategy from the US nuclear deterrent.

(d) *Decoupling NATO strategy from the US nuclear deterrent.* Even if all nuclear weapons and bases are removed from Europe, as long as the US is a nuclear power, the European NATO countries in a sense cannot avoid being associated with some form of strategic deterrence. The US nuclear commitment to Europe means that in some circumstances a war in Europe could escalate into a global nuclear confrontation. A longer-term goal, implicit in the rejection of nuclear weapons on principle, must include a 'decoupling' of the defence of Europe from the US nuclear deterrent. To this end, as well as insisting that the US should not use nuclear weapons against a conventional attack on Western Europe, European countries should ask the US not to threaten retaliation even to a Soviet nuclear attack on Europe.

There is already a substantial constituency for the first three steps in de-nuclearizing NATO. A no-first-use declaration followed by withdrawal of battlefield nuclear weapons would raise the nuclear threshold, while removing nuclear weapons from Europe would further reduce the risks of Europe becoming a theatre of nuclear war and provide openings for mutual arms reduction and constructive political initiatives. These arguments have a direct appeal in terms of European security interests. The fourth step, however, of decoupling NATO strategy from the US deterrent is one that few European members of NATO have yet been willing to contemplate.

There is, however, in addition to the argument from principle, a strategic case for seeking to avoid even this limited reliance on the US nuclear deterrent. The case against any form of nuclear deterrence includes the impossibility of securing permanently stable deterrence, and a judgement that a nuclear holocaust would be the worst outcome of a war. Any form of US nuclear commitment to Europe would make it more difficult to confine a European war to the conventional level.

Ultimately, of course, the European members of NATO could

not prevent American nuclear threats or indeed nuclear retaliation; and so long as it has over 200,000 ground troops in Europe, the US would be wary about promising never to use its nuclear weapons in a European war. Nevertheless, though this cannot but raise very challenging military and political questions for the alliance, European members should seek such an undertaking: a public agreement by the US that its nuclear forces have no place in *alliance* strategy.

2. De-nuclearizing NATO

It will not be easy to wean NATO away from its reliance on nuclear weapons, but in view of the strength of the peace movements in other NATO countries and of the attitudes of certain governments in NATO, an opportunity may exist for changing NATO from within. Historically, US nuclear forces have been stationed in Europe less as a form of American imposition than as a result of European pressure. Now, however, more European governments and leading politicians are calling on the US to negotiate nuclear arms reductions, and there are striking similarities in the policies of the social democratic parties in several NATO countries over questions such as no-first-use and the deployment of cruise and Pershing II.

Within the military, too, received strategic assumptions are increasingly being questioned and there is widespread concern to 'raise the nuclear threshold'. A non-nuclear Britain, acting in concert with like-minded goverments in other NATO countries, may be able to shift NATO policy decisively.

Such a fundamental revision of NATO strategy should enhance the security of Western Europe, whether or not the Soviet Union responded in kind. The Soviet Union would, however, be foolish not to reciprocate unilateral initiatives by NATO or by individual NATO members and, although the *arguments* for de-nuclearizing NATO do not depend on Soviet goodwill, the actual process would obviously be greatly assisted by genuine reciprocation.

Most members of the Alternative Defence Commission believe that Britain can best influence the situation by staying in NATO on the condition that NATO reconsiders its dependence upon a nuclear strategy. Britain would thus continue to participate in the common defence of Europe, while the alliance takes steps to move towards non-nuclear forms of defence.

If Britain simply decided to leave NATO, however, the reactions of other NATO countries to this could actually set back the prospects for a nuclear-free Europe. European members of NATO might see British withdrawal as an isolationist move and resent Britain seeming to use Western Europe as a buffer zone against Soviet attack without sharing the risks in Europe's defence. The US, aggrieved by its loss of important bases in Britain, might then be able to exert greater economic pressure on Britain by enlisting European support.

Worse still, if NATO overreacted to being weakened by Britain's departure – for instance, if West Germany built up its armed forces – this might alarm the Soviet Union afresh and heighten tension even further. Alternatively, if British withdrawal triggered the break-up of NATO, the repercussions might be more dangerous than the present situation: for instance, an isolationist US might turn itself into a nuclear 'Fortress Americana', immune to international pressures in favour of arms control, or West Germany and France might form a new nuclear axis.

Ultimately, peace in Europe requires the dissolution of the military blocs, yet an immediate British withdrawal from NATO, far from being a step in this direction, might be dangerously destabilizing, even precipitating a more hazardous realignment than at present.

3. *Negotiation with NATO*
Though immediate British withdrawal would be too drastic and its consequences too unpredictable, a non-nuclear Britain which sought to remain in NATO should be aware of the opposite danger – of failing to challenge NATO's nuclear policy. Little would be gained if NATO merely accommodated a member which resolutely refused to cooperate with any nuclear war planning – as it has already accommodated the more limited refusals of Canada and Norway to handle nuclear weapons in peacetime, without any significant impact upon NATO policies.

We attach special importance to our view that a non-nuclear Britain's membership of NATO should be strictly *conditional* and that some timetable would be necessary by which Britain could assess whether or not its conditions were being met. While Britain should dismantle its own nuclear arsenal as quickly as possible, a transition by NATO as a whole to a non-nuclear strategy would necessarily require complex negotiations and phasing.

The first step Britain should take is to identify other NATO members wishing to reduce NATO's reliance on nuclear weapons, and if possible to establish an anti-nuclear caucus within NATO. The precise approach to negotiations with NATO would be decided in consultation, but a unilateralist British government might argue for the following negotiating strategy.

(a) *To convene a special NATO conference* to communicate to NATO's political leaders that some members of NATO had resolved to reject nuclear weapons but wished to maintain their contributions to the collective defence of Western Europe.

(b) *To announce that the anti-nuclear members of NATO could not take part in any future exercises* which envisaged the use of nuclear weapons by NATO or cooperate in any way with NATO's nuclear forces.

(c) *To propose a timescale* for phasing out NATO's nuclear strategy.

All this involves a more fundamental and far-reaching rejection of nuclear policies than any NATO government has yet agreed. Britain may find allies willing to go only part of the way down this road; in which case, the prospects for de-nuclearizing NATO would be correspondingly poor. Britain, however, should remain firm in adhering to its nuclear disarmament proposals. If all else fails, a British withdrawal from the alliance following such discussions might at least gain a measure of understanding of its motives by its former NATO partners.

The top priority in ending NATO's reliance on nuclear weapons would be the adoption of a no-first-use policy. Britain would require a statement of intent on this and on the removal of cruise and Pershing II within a year of the NATO conference as a sign that progress was possible in meeting other conditions.

The next step would be the withdrawal of short-range battlefield nuclear weapons from Europe. Preferably, battlefield nuclear weapons might be withdrawn through negotiation, perhaps as part of a move towards a nuclear disengagement zone, such as the Palme Commission's proposal for a 300km-wide corridor along the East and West German borders. Failing this, however, NATO should remove these weapons unilaterally.

Unless substantial progress is made towards removing both battlefield and theatre nuclear weapons from Europe within a period of three years, Britain should consider withdrawing from the alliance.

Britain and the US could bilaterally agree a schedule for the removal from Britain of nuclear-related US forces – again we suggest a period of about three years.

The 'decoupling' of the US nuclear deterrent from the defence of Europe is inevitably the most problematic step involved in this policy. Many Europeans have a deep-seated fear that Western Europe cannot be defended without the US nuclear guarantee. Consequently, there is less support in Europe for 'decoupling' than for any other de-nuclearizing policy. Non-nuclear defence strategy for NATO would, of course, have to be jointly formulated. While Britain may propose its preferred argument for particular defensive postures and press for negotiated arms reductions in central Europe, it would have to be highly flexible in these matters. Indeed, it might have to make an increased contribution to the conventional defence of central Europe.

If progress towards de-nuclearizing NATO came to a standstill, Britain should first withdraw from the integrated military command structure while remaining on NATO's North Atlantic Council – a step taken by France in 1966. If NATO took further steps towards a non-nuclear strategy, Britain could resume full membership. Otherwise, it would have to complete its withdrawal from NATO. In that case, the possibilities of British nonalignment or of creating a non-nuclear Western European defence association would move to the centre of British policy.

Outside NATO

If Britain could not persuade NATO to take a non-nuclear stance, it would basically have two options: to be militarily independent, taking a non-aligned position between East and West, or to promote the formation of some kind of non-nuclear European defence association. These options in any case warrant consideration as alternatives to the policy of trying to change NATO from within.

1.   *British Non-alignment*

Non-alignment would involve British withdrawal from all military alliances and the pursuit of an independent defence policy. It also implies political independence from the great powers and a refusal to take sides in the cold war.

The most obvious model for Britain to follow in these circumstances would be Sweden which, over the last twenty years, has combined non-involvement in military alliances with an active foreign policy. Britain need not necessarily interpret neutrality as rigidly as Sweden has; for instance, non-alignment need not entail Britain leaving the EEC or seeking self-sufficiency in weapons production. But there is much to be learned from Sweden's international role. Sweden has been prominent in attempting to initiate disarmament agreements, in UN peace-keeping, and in mediation of international conflicts, while at the same time supporting the rights of developing nations. Thus, Sweden's traditional neutralism has grown into a positive stance of non-alignment and the promotion of international understanding and human rights.

Were Britain to follow a similar course, this could be a tremendous fillip to the peace movements of the other European members of NATO while, at government level, British withdrawal from NATO would force a reappraisal of the political and military situation in Europe. In favourable circumstances, such a striking departure from traditional assumptions could encourage the superpowers to reconsider their policies on disarmament and disengagement. Some members of the Commission therefore in any case favoured non-alignment (rather than conditional

membership of NATO). The majority of the Commission, however, concluded that British non-alignment should be accepted
only if Britain failed to shift NATO towards a non-nuclear
policy: on balance, the opportunity to change NATO policy
from within outweighed the attractions of greater freedom of
action.

2. *A Non-nuclear European Defence Organization*

A non-nuclear European defence organization would safeguard
Britain's links and commitments to Europe and maintain a
multinational defence in central Europe. The European connec-
tion would be especially valuable to Britain if it could not stay in
NATO, but European independence from the superpowers also
has the appeal of being a form of continental non-alignment.

Unlike British non-alignment, however, the creation of a non-
nuclear European defence organization may not be a feasible
option. Continental Western European countries may refuse to
contemplate mounting a credible conventional defence against
the Soviet Union without US support. Currently, European
countries contribute between 65 and 75 per cent of NATO-ready
forces in Europe. Naturally, the costs of defence would depend
upon the exact posture chosen. If Western Europe confined itself
to the aim of making an attack seem unlikely to be worth the
risks, this would limit the defence burden. If, however, the aim
was a decisive repulse of Soviet forces, then this would probably
require a conventional build-up.

A second obstacle to the formation of a non-nuclear association
would be the attitude of France. It would be difficult to conceive
of a credible Western European defence organization which did
not include France, but France is deeply committed to its
independent nuclear deterrent. Indeed, part of the official rationale for the French *force de frappe* is that it would be available to an
independent European defence organization.

Even if it were possible to form a non-nuclear European
defence organization, certain political dangers would need to be
weighed. Rather than helping to heal the current East-West
military divide, a Western European military bloc might recon-
stitute the division of Europe with a new rigidity. There would be

a newly established organization with a fresh political momentum behind it. And any conventional military build-up by this association would arouse new suspicions about possible European aspirations to become a third superpower. Indeed, such an organization might not only be seen as the expression of a 'European nationalism', it might actually become the focus for such a movement.

A non-nuclear association could try to allay these fears by adopting a strictly defensive stance. It could decide not to have an integrated military command but some looser arrangement, which would make it seem less like a military bloc which tends to function in peacetime as if it was at war. In that case, however, those countries with memories of being overrun by Hitler's troops are likely to be sceptical of a 'collective security' agreement which amounts to mere promises of help in the event of war. Certainly, unless British forces were irrevocably committed to mainland Europe, British guarantees of aid might not be reassuring.

All members of the Commission agreed that there would be little point in deliberately breaking up NATO in favour of an independent, non-nuclear Western European defence organization which at present is purely speculative and whose formation would certainly be a difficult and hazardous exercise. However, if the US blocked the attempt to de-nuclearize NATO, and there were strong European support for a non-nuclear defence organization, then this option may grow in force.

Conclusions

The members of the Commission agreed that a non-nuclear Britain cannot remain in NATO while NATO strategy remains committed to nuclear weapons. Most conclude that the best chance for general nuclear disarmament is pressure through NATO, staying in NATO to shift it to a non-nuclear strategy. NATO membership should, however, be conditional on NATO making progress towards ending its reliance on nuclear weapons. A minority favours Britain leaving NATO and pursuing an independent, non-aligned policy. If Britain stays in

NATO but fails to persuade it to a non-nuclear strategy, then Britain would have to consider either British non-alignment or the formation of a non-nuclear Western European defence organization.

4. Central Europe: Western Military Options

The security of Western Europe does not depend mainly, or even primarily, on military measures. Defence in many ways has to be subordinate to politics, especially in the political signals it sends. The current policies of both military blocs signal distrust and hostility; they are perceived as threatening and risk being provocative. A non-nuclear, non-provocative defence policy could reduce tension and effectively signal a commitment to disarmament.

In switching to a non-nuclear strategy, NATO would have clear political goals. It would hope that this might open the way to further changes, such as some reciprocation from the Soviet Union in withdrawing nuclear weapons, negotiated arms reductions, and the formal establishment of demilitarized zones or nuclear weapons-free zones.[1]

But while a non-nuclear defence policy should be oriented towards promoting disarmament, it must be credible in its own right as a defence policy, maximizing the military and political dissuasion to attack while minimizing the likelihood of the Soviet Union resorting to nuclear or chemical warfare if a war should break out.

This chapter looks at *military* options for the defence of Western Europe. We concentrate on relatively near-term measures which could be taken unilaterally by NATO if it was willing to phase out its reliance on nuclear weapons. Some of these options would also be open to a non-nuclear Western European defence organization independent of the US, although, without US finance, technology and troops, such an organization would be more limited in its range of choices. The possibility of NATO abandoning its integrated command structure is discussed in Chapter 5.

The Military Objective of Defence

What objectives should underlie NATO strategy in Europe? Broadly, we can distinguish between three different levels of military capability. At the lowest level would be a largely symbolic stance, including some policing functions, but in a war mainly serving to announce that aggression had taken place. This stance makes sense only if the main emphasis in defence is on non-military or para-military forms of resistance, such as we consider in Chapter 6. In this case, dissuasion against aggression would depend upon the costs of meeting popular resistance.

At the medium level, there are the Swedish and Swiss models of a 'high entry price' policy. This cannot count on defeating the full might of a major power but aims to deter attack by making it dangerously costly. This would be a military as well as a political deterrent. It is a reasonable stance for a neutral country which could not acquire the means to defeat a major power, and is therefore considered more fully in Chapter 5 in the context of British non-alignment. It is less appropriate for an alliance, however, as one of the main reasons countries join forces is to gain a higher level of insurance against defeat than they could achieve on their own.

The top level is the capacity to win a war. It implies a high investment of resources in defence; and since it envisages a highly destructive conventional war, it is extremely likely to prompt eventual escalation to the nuclear level.

The most satisfactory military policy in Europe is probably, therefore, something more potent than a 'high entry price' policy without aiming at a classical 'victory': that is, to ensure that Soviet forces could be arrested unless the Soviet government went to enormously destructive conventional lengths or escalated to the nuclear level. Such a policy might be reinforced by forms of fall-back resistance, in the case of an occupation, through guerrilla warfare or civil resistance (see Chapter 6).

Before considering in more detail what forms a non-nuclear

NATO strategy for Europe might take, we need to examine the context of NATO's European objectives.

THE POLITICAL CONTEXT FOR DEFENCE

1. *West Germany*

A collective system of defence enhances the deterrent and defensive capacity of each individual country. Nowhere is this more critical than where the military blocs border each other. The main battleground for NATO would be West Germany whose vulnerability actually puts some limits on the choice of defence policies for NATO in Europe. For instance, the existence of a multinational force on West German territory is a visible commitment by other countries that they will defend West German territory; it is therefore difficult to discuss reallocating NATO resources by withdrawing these troops.

West Germany is a highly industrialized and urban country. It has traumatic memories of the devastation of the Second World War. Out of a concern to limit a war being waged over West German territory, NATO has based its strategy on the concept of 'forward defence' – that is, the aim of holding the line near the East German frontier, rather than mounting a 'defence in-depth' and waging a war of attrition. NATO strategy at a conventional level has always been primarily defensive, though including an ability to counter-attack; and now, as we shall see, NATO is considering ways to wrest the initiative from the Soviet Union and to carry the battle deeper into Warsaw Pact territory.

2. *West Berlin*

A permanent solution to the problem of Berlin will have to be part of a wider political settlement. In the meantime, there is no ideal method of defending a city divided in half and surrounded by hostile troops. Limited conventional preparations and guerrilla resistance, or non-violent resistance, may be appropriate to the specific and limited threat of a Soviet takeover of the city. Political deterrence could also be strengthened, for example by locating an international organization in West Berlin. There remains, however, a strong political case for maintaining the American, British and French garrisons in West Berlin as a symbol of political and military commitment.

3. *Eastern European Countries Inside the Warsaw Pact*

The conflicts of interest within the Eastern bloc have military implications. For instance, the potential unreliability of Eastern European troops could influence the outcome of a conventional war in central Europe. Taking into account the historic resentments and traditional enmities and affinities of Eastern European countries, one study found that Polish, willingness to engage in combat operations against NATO forces in anything but a highly successful engagement is questionable at best', that the Czechoslovakians 'would be of almost no use to the Soviets', while the reliability of the Hungarian army would be 'minimal at best'.[2]

If it did launch an offensive, the Warsaw Pact might have to face popular resistance in the rear. While NATO countries tend to support popular movements to reform or challenge Soviet-style regimes, present nuclear strategy threatens to destroy apparatchik and dissident alike. Consequently it serves to cement the Eastern bloc in the face of a perceived Western threat. A clearly 'defensive' strategy would limit the military threat posed to Eastern European countries and would thus favour resistance inside the Soviet bloc if it came to a war.

Whether or not troops and civilians would rebel in time of war would depend on the circumstances. The likelihood of disaffection will be higher if Eastern European troops were required to take part in an offensive. Eastern European disaffection would also be more likely if NATO blunted an initial Soviet drive into West Germany.

4. *Political Goals*

It is clearly essential to reduce tension between NATO and the Warsaw Pact and the danger of war through miscalculation. This must include avoiding strategies which would put pressure on either side to take pre-emptive action in a crisis. In the longer term, the requirements of seeking disarmament should help to shape defence policy. For these reasons, we prefer a military posture which can be seen as strictly defensive, a strategy which is neither designed to nor capable of carrying out a major offensive against Eastern Europe and the Soviet Union, even in response to an invasion. Such a strategy need not, however, mean dispensing with the capacity to counter-attack enemy forces *within* NATO territory; such a capacity forms an integral part of defence.

CONVENTIONAL DEFENCE FOR WESTERN EUROPE

Options for the conventional defence of Western Europe can be grouped under three main headings.

1. Keep the present strategy of front-line defences.
2. Take the offensive by building up front-line forces and the capacity for conventional strikes in Warsaw Pact territory.
3. Shift to a strictly defensive strategy.

We have already noted the political objections to an offensive strategy. However, further discussion is needed of its military aspects.

1. *Keep the Present Strategy of Front-line Defences*

Present NATO strategy is based on 'forward defence', in which forces are massed as far forward as possible at the West German frontier. Present conventional defences in central Europe are strong enough to prevent an easy or quick Soviet victory and may therefore be an adequate deterrent to Soviet attack.

The effectiveness of present NATO forces could also be greatly increased: for instance, by stationing troops closer to their allocated wartime positions, increasing the numbers and improving the training of reservists and territorial army forces, employing mines and precision-guided munitions weapons more extensively, setting up obstacles near the border. There is plenty of scope for NATO to improve its capability without actually increasing the number of troops.

However, this policy would meet with objections from those who argue that, in view of Soviet conventional superiority, NATO needs to have the option of using nuclear weapons first. Current NATO strategy envisages the early use of battlefield nuclear weapons in the face of Soviet attack. Furthermore, the very existence of battlefield nuclear weapons might induce Warsaw Pact caution about massing its forces since troop concentrations are a natural target for these weapons. Pledging no-first-use of nuclear weapons and withdrawing battlefield nuclear weapons could therefore, it has been argued, undermine confidence in NATO's existing conventional defences.

Worries about Western weakness tend to be overstated. If conventional forces in central Europe are compared not just by numbers but by the quality of their equipment and training, and if the advantages of the defence are taken into account, the imbalances appear in a different light (see Appendix A). NATO has a higher proportion of professional troops than the Warsaw Pact and, despite considerable recent improvements in the latter's equipment, NATO equipment, on balance, remains superior.

Simply retaining the present arrangements for conventional frontier defence would miss the opportunity to rethink NATO's strategy. This is urgently necessary, not only politically but also militarily, where NATO has become caught in a trap of over-sophisticated 'gold-plated technology' which is often unreliable on the battlefield and requires extraordinary provisions for maintenance. Twice in September 1984, NATO was confronted with embarrassing evidence about its existing high technology. The first occasion had a direct bearing on NATO's readiness in central Europe: Texas Instruments had to recall microchips installed in a variety of weapons systems because they had been inadequately tested and might be defective. The second incident concerned the US navy: the US General Accounting Office found that a quarter of the US navy's Sidewinder and a third of its Sparrow air-to-air missiles were unserviceable for combat use because of defects or maintenance problems.

The present strategy can, however, be adapted to overcome these shortcomings. By making greater use of European territorial forces to augment the front-line troops, NATO could both reduce its dependence on reinforcements flown in from the US and also simplify its equipment. These territorial forces would be lightly armed and equipped with simpler and cheaper types of defensive weapons such as hand-held anti-tank and anti-aircraft missiles. They could be used in either a static or a mobile role. In a more static role, they could staff anti-aircraft batteries, guard installations and communications, lay minefields and hold prepared defensive positions. Exploiting their mobility, they could use their local knowledge to lay ambushes and harry the enemy. If they were deployed in front-line zones such as forests and built-up areas, this would release NATO armoured divisions to concentrate on the open corridors of land. In general, they could play a defensive and supplementary role in the rear.

Whereas the British territorial army is a part-time force, the West German territorial army is a mixture of conscripts, part-time volunteers and full-time professionals. An expansion of NATO territorial forces along similar lines would provide greater defensive depth and flexibility at a lower cost than building up the regular forces on the front-line.

At present, the West German government is totally opposed to partisan warfare in territory the enemy has occupied. It therefore envisages its territorial forces retreating with the regular forces, rather than remaining in place and creating pockets of armed resistance. It also aims to avoid putting urban areas at risk and therefore plans to make no military use of cities. There are good grounds for any government to hesitate before requiring from its people the sacrifice which could be involved in a determined territorial defence and a campaign of partisan resistance (we discuss its major disadvantages in the next chapter). West Germany might, however, consider more limited extensions of territorial defence. Where a country is as vulnerable to land attack as West Germany, the deterrent value of supplementing conventional frontier defence with territorial defence preparations may outweigh the danger of the additional destruction and suffering which may be involved. The existence of a defensive network of lightly armed territorial units – not capable by themselves of halting an armoured attack but able to disrupt communications and supplies and generally to harass – would greatly increase the difficulty of invading forces who could no longer concentrate solely on defeating NATO regular troops.

The burden of bolstering NATO's territorial forces would fall most heavily on West Germany. It would be extremely difficult to organize an effective multinational territorial force, and unless they are trained in West Germany, territorial soldiers from other countries would be more limited in the roles they could play. Other NATO countries may therefore have to increase their contribution to NATO's front-line defences in order to release West German forces for this expanded territorial role, and also show a willingness to strengthen their own territorial forces.

2. *Taking the Offensive*

Rather than buttress NATO's current forward defence with defensive, territorial preparations, NATO is preparing for strategies which would extend NATO's counter-attacking capability and take the war further into Warsaw Pact territory.

AirLand Battle is already US army doctrine. It 'breathes the spirit of the offence'. Its advocates argue that NATO conventional strategy has been too passive. They lay great emphasis on NATO seizing the initiative – not just defending the West German frontier but looking for points of Warsaw Pact vulnerability to attack. Under the AirLand Battle concept, NATO forces would want to be able to strike at Warsaw Pact troops well behind the frontier. A corps commander, who currently directs the war up to a range of about 25km, would then have a territory stretching about 150km into East Germany.

This strategy would require greater ability to manoeuvre and the use of 'Emerging Technology' to enable better monitoring, tracking and targeting of enemy troops and more precision-guided missiles. It would also require better coordination between ground and air forces; and the US army would also like the ground commander to have direct control of air support.

At the moment, AirLand Battle envisages the use of 'tactical nuclear and chemical weapons at an early stage and in enemy territory',[3] but a similar strategy could be pursued using solely conventional weapons, such as 'area-impact munitions' with a counter-force capability equivalent to a small nuclear explosion – up to 5 kilotons.

With such an offensive concept of defence, NATO would have less room for initiative in proposing force reductions. Indeed,

AirLand Battle would be more likely to herald a new conventional arms race.

Follow-on Force Attack, or Deep Strike as it is commonly known, was adopted by NATO in December 1984. Like AirLand Battle, it envisages two battles: one on the West German border where NATO would seek to resist the first thrust of the Soviet attack; the other – the deep battle – striking at reinforcements, in this case as deep into Warsaw Pact territory as the westernmost military districts of the Soviet Union. In particular, it would target logistical 'choke points' (such as bridges, road junctions and railway yards), troop concentrations, ammunition and fuel depots, airfields, and command, control, communication and information (C3I) facilities.

The idea is based on the understanding that Warsaw Pact forces are organized in echelons; if they attack it will be in waves. NATO, therefore, is seeking to cut off the Soviet front-line from reinforcements. The key military term is 'interdiction', defined as 'isolating or sealing off an area; denying the use of a route or approach'. NATO has always had a deep 'interdiction' strategy but, rather than rely on manned aircraft, Deep Strike, like AirLand Battle, will depend heavily on the use of emerging technologies – in particular 'target acquisition systems' and enormously powerful conventional 'area-impact munitions'. Unlike AirLand Battle, however, Deep Strike does not envisage NATO ground troops counter-attacking in Eastern Europe.

Deep Strike conceives of an 'integrated battlefield' where sophisticated surveillance and tracking equipment feed targeting information into a central computer which then guides the missiles. In contrast to AirLand Battle, which increases the power of the ground commander, Deep Strike retains centralized control of these strikes.

Deep Strike has been presented as a means of reducing reliance on battlefield nuclear weapons and thereby 'raising the nuclear threshold'. It is also seen as reducing the risk of a surprise Soviet attack by restraining Soviet attempts to mass forces. The argument here is that, in view of the reach of Deep Strike's tracking systems and the accuracy of its missile guidance systems, Soviet concentrations of troops would be put at risk.

Deep Strike could, however, have the reverse effect, lowering the nuclear threshold and increasing the risk of a Soviet pre-emptive attack. Even if NATO had removed its theatre nuclear weapons, Deep Strike would be destabilizing. It is also open to objection on technical, financial and arms control grounds, as well as being based on a dubious understanding of Warsaw Pact strategy.

Manned aircraft are too vulnerable to air defences to be the main vehicle of a Deep Strike strategy. Deep Strike therefore depends on the development of an array of new missiles and targeting systems which are far from proven. Individually, the elements which make up Deep Strike – the radar, the missile guidance, etc. – have not been thoroughly tested. Opportunities for unreliability will be multiplied when these are fitted together into a system, and especially when they have to be tried in battlefield conditions.

Not only is the technology involved in Deep Strike formidably complex, but the continued efficacy of the strategy would depend on NATO keeping one step ahead of the Warsaw Pact's counter-measures.

Current cost estimates for Deep Strike are probably extremely optimistic for a technology still under development. However, even its advocates expect that, in order to pay for Deep Strike, NATO countries would have to raise their defence spending by more than the 3 per cent per year real increase they have agreed as their target for the years up to 1986. Yet most NATO countries have fallen well short of this target, and even Britain does not intend to maintain this level of increase after 1986.

Since the strategy depends upon NATO front-line troops being able to hold an initial Warsaw Pact attack, NATO could not reallocate resources from its front-line defence for Deep Strike. Indeed, a fundamental military criticism of Deep Strike is that attacking follow-on forces would be in vain since the success or failure of a Soviet offensive would primarily depend on the achievements of the first echelon. Even the ESECS report, which promotes Deep Strike, contains a 'supporting paper' which casts doubt on the priority which should be given to Deep Strike. Christopher Donnelly envisages that a surprise Soviet attack would aim to get large-scale combat groups behind NATO lines as quickly as possible, on the first or second day of an invasion; there may well be no second echelon in East Germany for several days.[4]

Whatever the correct interpretation of existing Soviet strategy, it would be wrong to base NATO strategy on the assumption that a Soviet offensive would depend on such echeloning, and it could be fatal to divert resources from the most critical front-line battle.

Any strategy which depends on maintaining technological superiority can be opposed on arms control grounds for it is bound to lead to a 'race against technology', as one side seeks to combat the other side's counter-measures before they have even entered production. To the extent to which NATO would use dual-capable – nuclear and conventionally-armed – missiles for Deep Strike, Deep Strike would also hinder verification of arms control agreements.

The most critical objection to Deep Strike is that it would be destabilizing. Strategies that emphasize seizing the initiative encourage pre-emption. They make escalation more rapid and uncontrollable. AirLand Battle, with its emphasis on manoeuvre and counter-thrusts in Warsaw Pact territory, would increase Soviet fear of surprise attack, while Deep Strike, even if it employed only conventional missiles, would add considerably to NATO's capacity for 'surgical strikes' against Warsaw Pact defences. The Soviet Union in turn might respond to such strategies by developing its own capacity for surprise attack and also its own Deep Strike capability.

The idea that NATO could accurately track and target force movements hundreds of miles into Warsaw Pact territory is bound to alarm the Soviet military, especially while NATO retains any nuclear weapons or while the defence of Western Europe is coupled with the US nuclear arsenal. Even as purely conventional strategies, however, both AirLand Battle and Deep Strike may create the impression that NATO is willing to strike first, and in a situation of crisis may actually tempt NATO to do so. At the same time, they would give the Soviet Union more incentive to strike first than would a more defensive posture. In just the same way that the Soviet Union's strategy of carrying the war into NATO territory appears offensive to NATO, so Soviet strategists might pay more attention to NATO's offensive conventional *capability* than to its avowedly defensive *intentions*.

Far from raising the nuclear threshold, the immediate danger is heightened by the existence of dual-capable missiles. Some of the missiles proposed for conventional deep strikes, such as the improved Lance (range 240 miles), cruise and Minuteman missiles,[5] are also nuclear-capable. Their use could be misinterpreted by the Soviet Union as the start of a nuclear attack.

The strategies of AirLand Battle and Deep Strike raise the whole question of the role of counter-attack in NATO's defences of central Europe. While there is a strong military case for NATO to keep some capacity for counter-attack – in particular to disrupt Soviet supplies and reinforcements – these measures should be sufficiently limited in scale to signal their purely defensive intent. If Eastern Europe is a potential friend rather than an enemy, NATO would be best advised to limit destruction of Eastern European territory, while if NATO appeared to be launching a counter-attack against Eastern Europe, this could have a unifying effect on Soviet satellite states and their forces may fight seriously in self-defence.

Counter-attacks should therefore concentrate not only on strictly military targets but, as far as possible, on Soviet – rather than Eastern European – military targets or lines of communications. So as not to appear a threat to the peoples of Eastern Europe, this would best be done not by ground or missile attacks but either by attacking from the air or infiltrating specialized sabotage teams into Warsaw Pact territory.

3. *Purely Defensive Strategies*
If a primary purpose of restructuring NATO forces and strategy is to promote disengagement, disarmament and the eventual dismantling of the military blocs in Europe, then there is a strong political case for adopting weapons and deployments which denote a clearly defensive stance. Ideally, this would require a combination of weapons, deployment and strategy which indicates that no offensive action is intended or possible.

No weapon is in itself purely defensive. Even anti-tank and anti-aircraft missiles can be used to help an attack. However, the defensive character of the strategy should be clear if the weapons systems associated with offence – such as tanks, ground attack aircraft and long-range bombers – were kept clearly limited, and forces were dispersed within their own territory.

The political advantages of a defensive strategy are plain to see. The question is: would it be militarily credible?

Most purely defensive strategies aim to enhance the natural advantages of the defender with extensive use of precision-guided missiles and communications and intelligence-gathering techniques. Some of these systems are similar to those proposed for Deep Strike, but they would operate over shorter ranges (50km or less), are cheaper and often have been better tested.

Precision-guided missiles (PGMs) promise to be highly cost-effective: an anti-tank missile, such as the Milan (costing £7,000 in 1982) or the TOW (£2,000 in 1982), may destroy a tank costing many times as much, or an anti-aircraft missile, such as the hand-held Blowpipe (costing £15–20,000 in 1982), may bring down an aircraft. Nevertheless, there are also grounds for caution. The support equipment associated with an anti-tank missile can be expensive. Some PGMs may prove less reliable in battle than they have in tests. Some are difficult to use and are useless at night or in fog. Above all, military technology and military tactics never stand still. Whenever a weapon is developed which gives one side an advantage, the adversary is bound to look for ways of overcoming that. In the case of anti-tank missiles, as well as technical counter-measures – such as smoke-screens, electronic counter-measures and tougher tank armour – they could lead to changes of tactics such as tanks advancing only after massive artillery fire or air attack, or surprise attacks before the defences are mobilized.

While it is too early to be confident that PGMs have given the defence a permanent and decisive advantage, they do offer NATO new defensive possibilities.

Here we shall consider two basic types of defensive strategies utilizing the new technologies – one based on a variety of emerging technologies, the other on portable PGMs.

One defensive strategy, associated in Britain with the 'Just Defence' group, calls for a defensive belt in West Germany. As an illustration, one of its publications depicts a scheme where the first 4km on the western side of the border would be seeded with sensors in peacetime – seismic, acoustic, infra-red and chemical sensors to detect the vibration, sound, heat or exhaust gases of a tank incursion. Overhead, a satellite would scan the general area for early warning of offensive troop movements, while remotely piloted vehicles with TV cameras would keep the border itself under surveillance. All this information would be fed back into computerized command centres. On the first indication of attack, mines would be fired into this 4km zone. Motor cycle and infantry anti-tank and anti-aircraft missile launchers would be stationed in the next 2km band, backed up to a depth of about 20km by laser-guided or radar-controlled missiles. In addition, small squads of highly mobile troops, armed with missiles to give them maximum firepower, would be used against forces which either breached the forward zone of defence or parachuted behind it.[6]

This defensive belt concept is an illustration of how emerging technology could be employed as part of an unambiguously defensive strategy. It does not, however, amount to a battle-plan for a whole army. For instance, if the Warsaw Pact attacked not with a tank offensive but with an artillery barrage, or even missiles, this frontier defence would be quickly overwhelmed. Indeed, this kind of frontier defence could even be accused of *attracting* heavy firepower, perhaps including a tactical nuclear attack.

Like Deep Strike, such a defence would entail major dependence upon technology at the very boundaries of innovation which is often unproven and may be prone to obsolescence in the face of technical or tactical counter-measures.

At the other extreme, Horst Afheldt[7] advocates a purely defensive stance which dispenses altogether with frontier defence. He argues that frontier defence creates too many targets and is liable to escalation. Instead, there could be a network of defensive commando units throughout West Germany equipped with anti-tank weapons, mines and light infantry weapons. In addition there might be surface-to-air missiles for air cover. To cover West Germany, 10,000 units of these 'techno-commandos' – a total of 360,000 highly trained soldiers – would be needed to wage a war of attrition against a tank offensive and to lead opposition to landings by aircraft, plus reserves. Existing West German forces are already large enough to meet the needs of this strategy, but it would also be possible for troops from other NATO countries to be allocated their own patch to defend which they would get to know in advance.

The techno-commando units would have specific, well-defined tasks and would therefore depend less on a centralized command structure. They would avoid set-piece battles and would not fight in urban areas – Afheldt envisages non-violent resistance and non-cooperation in the cities and towns depriving the invaders of any military advantage if they chose to occupy them. Afheldt's strategy of attrition, in which he estimates that each commando unit would knock out three tanks, seems more realistic than aiming to hold a major tank attack with anti-tank weapons.

The most serious objections to this strategy arise from its lack of frontier defence. Not only is this likely to make it unacceptable on political grounds, but it would create other problems too. Minor incursions or border incidents could not be responded to militarily. Without being able to hold an attack, even briefly, there would be less time to try and use international diplomacy, on the one hand, or mobilize for war, on the other. This in-depth dispersed defence might in time wear down an attack, but it could not halt an advance early and counter-attacks to regain territory require the ability to concentrate one's own troops.

If the particular schemes advanced by Just Defence and Afheldt are not complete defence policies for NATO, they do indicate the kind of direction in which NATO could move once it had renounced nuclear strategy. There is no reason, for instance, why NATO could not retain its strategy of forward defence but rely on in-depth defences to fight a war of attrition if the front-line was breached. Such in-depth preparations would be unequivocally defensive and non-provocative but could significantly enhance deterrence.

Again, the kind of defensive belt proposed by Just Defence could be incorporated into NATO strategy. It would lend itself to the establishment of a military disengagement zone along the German border. NATO could unilaterally declare such a zone, perhaps extending 80km into West German territory, from which it would remove all major conventional weapons. An efficient surveillance system combined with small mobile units equipped with portable short-range weapons would then reduce the fear of surprise attack. If the Warsaw Pact responded by establishing a similar zone on its side of the border, this would represent a major step in the reduction of tension.

In general, then, we are not proposing a single grand scheme for the defence of Western Europe but calling on NATO to incorporate vital strategic insights from existing strategy and from new proposals into an unmistakably defensive strategy. What is important is less the technology, or the details of deployment, than the determination to fashion a military posture which reflects the alliance's defensive intentions.

The adoption of a strictly defensive strategy would call into question the deployment of certain types of weapons, in particular tanks and bomber aircraft or long-range missiles.

Tanks have two roles: to oppose other tanks, where PGMs may be tactically effective and cost-effective substitutes, and to provide both mobility and firepower. A defensive strategy would want to restrict the number of tanks but, if a limited counter-attacking capability is an essential part of defence, then tanks cannot be ruled out altogether.

Bomber aircraft and long-range missiles, targeted on enemy territory, do not fit in easily with a defensive strategy. While there are clear military advantages in being able to destroy enemy aircraft on the ground and to disrupt enemy lines of communication, the ability to do this can be perceived as evidence of a willingness to strike first and it could also increase the Soviet Union's incentive to strike first. In order to reduce tension and the possibility of war by miscalculation, it may make more sense to concentrate on a purely defensive air defence – a combination of surface-to-air missiles, anti-aircraft guns and fighter planes at higher altitudes.

CONCLUSIONS

The basic aim of NATO in central Europe should be to seek a 'defensive balance': that is, it should not aim to match the conventional might of the Warsaw Pact but, taking account of the defender's advantages in war, aim at being able to frustrate a Soviet offensive. As trends in weaponry, especially in the development of precision-guided missiles, may currently increase the defender's advantages, militarily, the time could be ripe for this kind of rethink.

A strictly defensive stance would not only serve to further tension-reducing and arms control measures, but it would also maximize the political deterrence to attack. The Soviet Union would find it more difficult to cement the Warsaw Pact in the absence of an apparent Western military threat. To launch an attack on Western Europe would imperil the relationships between the Soviet Union and other Pact members, and between Soviet-style regimes and the peoples of Eastern Europe.

Militarily, however, an entirely defensive strategy has severe disadvantages if it fails to avert war. West Germans would find it difficult to accept that the war should be fought on their territory without NATO being able to disrupt Soviet reinforcements. Some compromise is needed between a purely defensive posture and a posture with greater counter-attacking, and therefore offensive, capability. Fortunately, there is scope for compromise. The essential criterion is that any changes in NATO conventional policy should not increase its offensive capability but provide an evident base for shifting towards a more clearly defensive stance if political conditions become favourable.

If the precise military strategy to be adopted by a non-nuclear NATO has to remain open to negotiation, certain guidelines can be established.

1. It is necessary to retain some element of frontier defence, but this should not be so great as to appear threatening.

2. If present NATO conventional force levels do not seem adequate in the absence of nuclear weapons, they should be augmented by provisions for territorial and in-depth defence rather than by a conventional build-up at the front or by offensive strategies such as AirLand Battle or Deep Strike.

3. Numbers of tanks, long-range bombers and long-range missiles should be kept to a minimum, and if some capability to attack Warsaw Pact airfields and lines of communication is required, this should be strictly confined to military targets and preferably Soviet forces.

4. NATO should be sceptical about relying on unproven technology.

5. To reduce the risk of the Soviet Union using battlefield nuclear weapons, there should be a dispersed deployment of the territorial and in-depth forces and no military use should be made of cities.

5. National Defence: British Military Options

This chapter concentrates on choices in planning a military defence of Britain alone, as opposed to those strategies which focus on a common defence of central Europe. Although most members of the Commission would prefer to stay in NATO, we need to consider how Britain would defend itself if this policy failed and NATO could not be won to a non-nuclear strategy.

First, this chapter looks at the defence policies of three independent European neutrals who do not rely on nuclear weapons: Sweden, Switzerland and Yugoslavia. Obviously, Britain could not simply copy any of these examples, but it can learn from them.

Then we consider the role of different elements in a defence strategy for Britain: conventional frontier-based defence, the less orthodox in-depth 'territorial defence', which demands less sophisticated weapons technology and relies more on part-time soldiers, and 'partisan resistance' which may be relevant when an invader has occupied part of one's territory. In Chapter 6, we discuss methods of resistance to an occupying force.

CASES OF INDEPENDENT NON-NUCLEAR DEFENCE

For Sweden, Switzerland and Yugoslavia, the main adversary they have feared since the Second World War has been the Soviet Union. In the case of Sweden and Switzerland, the main threat is seen not as a full-scale military occupation but the seizure of areas of strategic importance during a major European war. Yugoslavia, however, particularly since the Soviet invasion of Czechoslovakia in 1968, has concentrated more on deterring direct attack than on the dangers arising from a wider war.

Naturally, these countries cannot match the military might of a superpower. Nevertheless, while they would, in the event of war, look for help and allies, they try to conceive of their defence independently. Therefore, they have concentrated on making their countries hard to conquer. They aim to deter attack by being able to exact a 'high admission price' from any invader.

The idea of a 'nation in arms' is common to all three countries. It is part of a tradition of armed neutrality which has helped to keep Sweden and Switzerland out of war for nigh on 170 years, while in Yugoslavia it arose out of the experience of partisan resistance in the Second World War. Each country has an 'inflatable army' – that is, upon attack they will be prepared instantly to expand their standing armies. This requires widespread military training – including conscription and refresher courses – and a system of local militias through which to mobilize. Beyond this, however, there are important distinctions between the three countries.

Table I: *Comparison of Sweden, Switzerland, Yugoslavia and Britain*

	Sweden	Switzerland	Yugoslavia	Britain
Population	8,380,000	6,500,000	23,100,000	56,000,000
Total armed				
forces	65,650	20,000	239,700	325,909
of which				
conscripts	47,850	18,500	154,000	nil
Period of				
conscription	10 months (average)	17 weeks	15 months	
Reserves	735,000	605,000	500,000	284,463
Para-military	500,000	480,000	3–5 million	
Military spending (for 1982)				
per capita	$379	$314	$132	$436
as % of GDP/GNP	3.6	2.1	5.2	5.3

Source: *The Military Balance, 1984–85*, International Institute for Strategic Studies.

Sweden aims to put up a substantial frontier defence, devoting over half its defence budget to the navy and airforce. Its impressive airforce is unambiguously defensive. Out of about 410 combat aircraft, it has no long-range bombers and is primarily geared towards interception (it has twice as many air-defence squadrons as bomber/ground-attack). The navy concentrates on coastal defence. It is equipped with twelve submarines, two destroyers and thirty-four fast attack craft as well as mine-layers, mine-sweepers and coastal patrol craft, and its firepower is augmented by shore-based artillery. The army stresses mobility and relies heavily on tanks – although small local units could maintain a stubborn resistance, their role is subsidiary except in coastal defence and the whole strategy is geared less to waging a war of attrition than to pushing back an invader.

Today, the most likely threat is seen not as a full-scale military occupation but as the seizure of areas of strategic importance by either side during a major European war. Frontier defence is therefore the militarily appropriate counter. In the case of a full-scale occupation, strong frontier defences would deny an invader an easy foothold in the country as well as gaining the time needed for the reserve army to be mobilized. Sweden would reckon to mobilize 10 per cent of the population within seventy-two hours; each reservist is therefore obliged to take part in eleven- to forty-day refresher courses five times between the ages of twenty and forty-seven.

Sweden has a concept of 'total defence' not confined to military preparations. Its civil defence programme aims to provide deep shelters for the whole population. Economically, it has taken measures to meet the problems of disruption of supply, for example by stockpiling food, fuel and various strategic materials. Sweden also takes into account the defence implications of major civilian projects: the Kiruna-Narvik motorway, for instance, was approved only after plans were added showing how it could be blown up if an invader sought to make use of it. Early in 1984 a government commission on 'complementary forms of resistance' recommended that forms of non-military resistance, such as civil resistance to an attempted occupation, should be more fully incorporated into Sweden's defence preparations with a permanent government commission to coordinate planning.

Switzerland has a part-time army with an officer corps of 1,500 regular soldiers; conscripts serve only seventeen weeks. Within forty-eight hours of an attack, 10 per cent of the Swiss population should be mobilized. They are kept in a state of readiness by periodic refresher courses and manoeuvres in their local areas; some 400,000 reservists each year do refresher training. Switzerland has a fairly substantial airforce of 310 combat aircraft, but its role would always be subordinate to the army. While some frontier defence would be maintained, not least to provide time to mobilize the reserves, and although the army has tank units to carry out counter-attacks, the primary defence strategy would be to disperse static infantry units to hold key positions. Once deployed, there would be a greater troop density in Switzerland than anywhere else in Europe, although one consequence of having so many men under arms is that they are likely to have inferior equipment.

Like Sweden, Switzerland has a major civil defence programme, including fall-out shelters in private houses, and an economic defence programme of stockpiling. It does not envisage its citizens' army waging a guerrilla war against occupation but, again like Sweden, views non-violent civil resistance as a complementary form of struggle.

Yugoslavia has more reason to fear great power attack, or attack with superpower support, outside the context of a European war. As a result, it lays great stress on defence in-depth, drawing on local territorial defence forces to supplement the Yugoslav People's Army. Unlike Switzerland, Yugoslavia explicitly plans for *indefinite* partisan resistance if the country is occupied. Indeed, the constitution goes so far as to make it illegal for a government to capitulate in the face of invasion. In view of the partisans' record of fierce resistance in the Second World War, the Yugoslavs' determination never to surrender is a credible deterrent.

All Yugoslavs are legally obliged to go through a basic training both in military aspects of defence and in protection measures. The republics and communes that make up Yugoslavia, and even some large industrial enterprises, organize territorial defence units locally, while schools include weapons training as part of the curriculum. As well as periods of conscription and refresher courses, the training system includes bodies such as the Rifle Federation and the radio hams' organization. In this way, Yugoslavia would hope to involve as much as 70 to 80 per cent of the population in various forms of resistance.

Against an attack by an Eastern European state with Soviet backing – Bulgaria, for instance – Yugoslavia would expect to mount a successful frontier defence. The army has backing from an airforce with some 420 combat aircraft, while the navy would defend Yugoslavia's long coastline. It has seven submarines, two frigates and three corvettes, but its main strength is in fast attack craft, mine-sweeping and mine-laying vessels.

Against a Soviet attack, the regular army would hope to hold the attack during mobilization; it is claimed that half the territorial defence force could be mobilized within six hours and the rest within twenty-four hours. The army would then retreat from the border regions, but continue to wage an active defence in-depth with heavy armour as long as possible. In occupied areas, the army would transform itself into a more lightly armed body waging partisan warfare alongside territorial defence units.

Alongside its military preparations, Yugoslavia has a civil defence force of 2 million when mobilized. This would try to protect and aid the civilian population in the course of what would probably be a very destructive war.

The British Situation

The nature and size of Britain's armed forces – in particular the navy – have been shaped by its imperial past. Since the Second World War, British defence policy has for the first time been closely integrated with the defence of Western Europe. If, however, a non-nuclear Britain withdrew all its forces from Europe and withdrew from NATO's integrated military command structure, this would require a fundamental rethink of defence strategy.

As Britain on its own cannot expect to be able to repulse the conventional forces of either of the superpowers, its basic choice would be between a military defence which aimed to deter attack by exacting a 'high admission price' or a policy which exerted primarily non-military pressures on a potential aggressor. We consider the possibilities of non-violent civil resistance in Chapter 6. As there is not likely to be widespread support for trusting in non-violent resistance as a defence policy until there are better prospects for agreed conventional disarmament, the more immediately realistic choice seems to be to devise a defensive deterrent, a 'high admission price' strategy.

The advantages of defensive deterrence are clear: it is conducive to good relations with other countries, removes any excuse for a pre-emptive strike by a potential enemy, and is compatible not only with nuclear disarmament but with limitation of various kinds of conventional weapons. In renouncing long-range missiles and bombers while retaining ground-attack aircraft, Sweden has shown how a primarily defensive policy can make provision for limited counter-attacking operations. If an independent Britain wanted to be able to attack an invasion fleet still in harbour or sabotage crucial facilities in enemy territory, this could still fit in with a non-provocative defensive posture. The essence of defensive deterrence is that it seeks to deter an attacker but does not appear to pose a threat.

In developing a defensive deterrent based on the 'high admission price' idea, Britain should not simply follow the example of Sweden, Switzerland or Yugoslavia. Each country has to take into account its own particular circumstances. Britain is a rather crowded and urbanized island a long way away from the superpowers. It has maintained highly professional armed forces equipped with sophisticated technology and has rarely imposed conscription.

The two main types of scenario for attacks on Britain are: (a) in a European war, either of the great powers might try to destroy military bases and facilities, such as ports and airports, or might try to seize these facilities – perhaps for their own use, perhaps just to prevent the other side using them; or (b) Soviet forces, having overrun other European countries – on the one side Norway and Denmark or on the other Western Europe up to the

Channel — might seek to occupy Britain. An invasion such as this would probably be preceded by a blockade.

Against these types of threat, Britain has a range of non-nuclear counter-measures. Militarily, it could rely on frontier-based conventional defence or territorial in-depth defence, but it could also adopt para-military forms of resistance such as guerrilla warfare or methods of non-armed resistance such as sabotage and non-violent civil resistance. Various elements of defence can be combined into an effective policy.

1. *Frontier-based Conventional Defence*

As an island, Britain enjoys certain advantages in defence. Since the advent of long-range missiles and bombers, the sea is a less effective barrier against destruction than it was but the problems of an invasion remain considerable. A strong British navy and airforce could therefore exact a formidable price from an attacking force, whether it was aiming at strategic seizure of certain areas during a war or intending a full-scale invasion.

The aim of a frontier-based conventional defence is to let through as little as possible or, if faced by clearly superior forces, to inflict serious losses on enemy ships and aircraft. These aims would imply a substantial modern navy and airforce. Current British defence planning sees the defence of Britain taking place primarily on the West German frontier and to a lesser extent on NATO's northern flank in Norway and Denmark, not on the frontiers of the UK itself. Therefore, it would be necessary to augment and restructure current conventional forces in various ways to provide a credible conventional defence.

Air defence. The air defence of Britain has been a low priority. As Minister of Defence, Mr Nott divulged that until recently more was spent on defending the fleet against air attack than on defending Britain itself. In the short term, the surface-to-air missiles (SAMs) and fighter squadrons now based in Germany might be brought to Britain, but generally a British-centred defence would have to lay greater emphasis on combat aircraft and SAMs.

At the moment, the RAF has thirteen strike/attack squadrons, five close-support squadrons and eight interceptor squadrons. A primarily defensive posture would favour fighter/interceptors and cut back heavily on strike aircraft. In doing this, the RAF would have to avoid the trap of 'gold-plated' technology – that is, over-refining designs by trying to squeeze in too many extra features. This usually leads to greatly increased costs in production and therefore fewer planes being acquired. These planes tend to be less reliable, to require more maintenance and to make new demands on crews which, in turn, means that fewer people can actually fly the planes and so more time and money has to be put into training.

The Harrier jump-jet is a good example of a cost-effective, high-technology plane whose design has not been over-complicated. Unfortunately, the Tornado programme, the RAF's most expensive ever procurement programme, is quite the reverse. The RAF is acquiring two versions of this multi-role combat aircraft – an interdictor/strike (IDS) plane, followed by an Air Defence Variant (ADV). In fact, the Tornado's roles are rather limited: as a ground-support aircraft it is too expensive to be risked against low-value targets; as a fighter it lacks thrust and manoeuvreability. Since 1980, three prototypes and seven operational models of Tornado have crashed, casting some doubt on its avionics and on the burden it places on its crew.

In future, simplicity should be the keynote of aircraft design, producing more models designed for a single purpose and at a lower unit cost.

Naval defence. The navy would need drastic restructuring; it is quite unsuited for a defence centred on the British Isles. Large surface vessels are not only expensive but vulnerable as was demonstrated all too plainly in the Falklands conflict when two Type 42 frigates, HMS *Sheffield* and HMS *Coventry*, were sunk. If the emphasis shifts to coastal defence, fast attack craft, mine-sweeping and mine-laying vessels and submarines are more appropriate.

Even if Britain moves away from having a high seas battle fleet, there is, however, a case for retaining some frigates – to cope with rough seas in the eastern Atlantic and North Sea, or in case

British territorial limits are challenged by other warships, or to provide some naval protection to shipping. Although one might rely largely on land-based aircraft and submarines to take a toll of an invasion fleet, the existence of a force of surface ships would be a clear signal of commitment to a naval defence. Overall, however, resources would be better allocated by reducing the number of ocean-going ships and strengthening off-shore protection.

If Britain concentrates on coastal defence, it will still need anti-submarine warfare capability. Its three anti-submarine warfare carriers may not be the appropriate way of maintaining this capability. By concentrating several functions in one ship, not only has efficiency been lost but a new high-value target has been created. Moreover, this valuable target is actually more vulnerable than smaller, faster ships and needs a task force group of other ships to protect it. To counter submarines more efficiently, Britain could choose either a combination of submarines and land-based aircraft or smaller surface ships – cruisers, destroyers and frigates – with anti-submarine warfare capability.

Ground forces. If Britain adopts a frontier-based defence, the role of ground forces would be secondary, but the ability to defeat a moderate-sized attacking force would be crucial in deterring attempts to seize territory for strategic purposes in the context of a European war. Also, if the Soviet Union was weighing the costs of an all-out invasion, an efficient British ground force could alter the balance.

As an enemy might try to land at many points, Britain would need a highly mobile force, but would need to take special measures to defend particularly vulnerable points, especially in view of the likelihood of airborne assaults designed to secure airfields, ports and communication centres. A regular army relying entirely on mobility could be spread too thinly or arrive too late. Therefore, there would be a need for some more localized static defences of key facilities, organized by units of the regular army (or the marines or the RAF) and drawing for reinforcements on regular reserves or on the territorial army. A force of marines might be involved in the protection of oil rigs. It would also be needed in any attempt to recapture, say, the Shetlands if they were seized by a superpower for strategic purposes.

In general, an independent British defence policy based on frontier defence would cut present personnel levels for the regular army and rely more heavily on reserves in the event of invasion.

2. *In-depth Territorial Defence*

In-depth defence can be carried out in several ways: by regular troops and reservists, by part-time volunteer forces like the territorial army, by a 'citizens' army' based on a system of universal conscription, or by local citizens' militias based on some system of universal military training. In practice, most systems use a mix of regular troops (or at least professional officers and NCOs) and conscripts, plus local defence forces and civil defence bodies.

According to current British military planning, the territorial army would be expected to provide between a quarter and a third of the army's mobilized strength in war, yet it costs only 4.4 per cent of the army's budget. Spending on the TA needs to be increased, however, if it is to become a larger and more effective fighting force.

The TA is currently undergoing expansion, but at the moment is 4,500 short of its theoretical complement of 76,000 and is unlikely to reach the target of 86,000 by 1990. It attracts only a small number of former regular soldiers – about 10 per cent of its membership – and its high turnover means that only about two-thirds of its members have completed minimum training. New incentives are needed to encourage people to join; more thorough training is needed for which employers will require compensation for periods of leave taken; and new equipment is also needed.

Even with this extra outlay, however, territorial defence would remain relatively cheap and has certain military advantages. It may be better able to counter dispersed airborne landings than mobile regular forces and, as it implies troop dispersal, it minimizes the likelihood of an enemy using battlefield nuclear weapons.

It does have military limitations, however. Territorial units cannot halt an armoured attack or drive out an invasion force, though they can slow it down. Although a territorial in-depth defence might include the use of anti-tank and anti-aircraft missiles, in the face of armoured divisions on the ground and dive-bombing from the air, territorial soldiers are likely to become demoralized. Territorial warfare might also result in very great suffering for the civilian population and also destruction of economic resources. In general, most of England, South Wales and the Lowlands of Scotland are too urban and densely populated to make in-depth defence attractive. It is a strategy more suited to the scattered population and formidable terrain of, for example, Switzerland.

Territorial defence for Britain, then, should be a *supplement* to a frontier-based conventional defence, rather on the lines of Sweden. Lightly armed and not very highly trained territorial forces would have more credibility as an *additional* problem facing invading troops who also had to contend with well-armed and well-trained regular soldiers. In this case, Britain might aim for a territorial force of between 100,000 and 250,000 part-time soldiers – the actual number would have to be decided according to the strategy envisaged. If the territorials' main function is to hold key points as long as possible, larger numbers may be needed than if they adopt partisan hit-and-run tactics aimed at cutting communication lines or harassing troops in the rear.

3. *Partisan Resistance*

Territorial defence overlaps with partisan resistance. The main distinction is that territorial defence, as in Switzerland, implies a willingness to stand and fight – to yield every yard at a cost to the invading forces – whereas partisans would continue the fight in occupied territory using means such as ambushes and sabotage, making swift strikes and then tactically withdrawing and regrouping.

Training for territorial defence and partisan warfare might well overlap. Both imply learning how to handle a rifle and a machine-gun, to use simple anti-tank missiles, and to lay mines and blow up bridges or railway lines. Territorial defence, however, suggests slightly heavier firepower and a greater commitment to 'dig in', whereas partisans rely much more on their mobility.

Here it is possible to envisage two branches of a territorial defence organization, receiving slightly different training and equipped with slightly different weapons – one concentrating on static defence, the other on hit-and-run tactics. In the next chapter we consider the possibility of indefinite military resistance through guerrilla warfare. Here we are thinking of a fairly short timespan, before either the invaders are repelled or the British government surrenders. In this situation, it would be feasible for partisan troops to hide during the day and act as uniformed troops when the opportunity arose. The case for reserving armed resistance to soldiers in uniform is that, if caught, they should be recognized as 'prisoners of war', and there would be less likelihood of invaders undertaking reprisals against civilians if a clear distinction is kept between combatant and non-combatant.

4. *Conscription*
Britain is exceptional in not having conscription. A non-nuclear defence of Britain by itself does not necessitate conscription, and Britain's current highly professional armed forces do not desire it. Nevertheless, there are arguments that Britain's defences would benefit from it.

At a time when nuclear disarmament indicated Britain's peaceful intent, the introduction of conscription would underline Britain's resolution to control its own affairs and resist aggression. Conscription would also be one way of building up a pool of trained reservists. Another set of arguments is that conscription is inherently more democratic – broadening the range of people within the army or, if it was part of a citizens' militia system, being a more decentralized and participatory form of organization.

Conscription is not necessary to achieve these goals, however. The reorganization of British defence would not require conscription to signal Britain's continuing will to resist, and diverting professional soldiers to the training of people with little aptitude and enthusiasm for the military may be judged inefficient. In terms of democracy, there are other ways of broadening the social base of the forces, and also of the territorial army. Nor would conscription necessarily democratize army structures: most conscript armies retain an élite of career soldiers. A system of citizens' militia may be decentralized yet still the authority to conscript would extend the central state's power over its subjects.

5. *A Nationally-based European Defence*

The kind of defence policies considered in this chapter would be equally relevant to the defence of a non-aligned Britain and to the defence of Europe if NATO abandoned its integrated military command structure and moved towards a looser alliance based on national defence policies. This would replace the goal of holding a Soviet attack at or near the West German frontier with the concept of cumulative attrition and harassment of Soviet forces, each country providing a kind of 'hedgehog' defence.

This type of defensive arrangement would have political advantages in surmounting the division of Europe into opposed military and political blocs, but it could not expect to defeat a really major Soviet attack. It mainly relies on each country defending itself tenaciously and continuing to resist after military defeat – either by partisan methods, or by non-violent civil resistance. Any country attacked would, however, receive military or financial assistance from unoccupied allies who would also have agreed to aid resistance to occupation (for instance, by harbouring refugees, publishing and broadcasting on behalf of the resistance and playing host to a government-in-exile).

CONCLUSIONS

A non-nuclear defence of a non-aligned Britain outside NATO has to be realistic about what it could achieve. It could not expect militarily to repel a full-scale attack by a major power but it could hope to deter such an attack by showing that an attack would cost the invader more than it was worth.

The defence of Britain should combine several elements. As an island, a military defence should involve strengthening naval and air defences. Despite cuts in the past, the navy and airforce are likely to remain strong into the 1990s, but would need to be restructured in an unambiguously defensive way – cutting down drastically on ocean-going ships and strike aircraft. The costs of high-technology weapons systems are rising steeply and Britain may well not be able to keep these up in future. In general, British forces should avoid the kind of over-complicated technology which tries to combine several roles in one weapons system and instead favour acquiring greater numbers of single-purpose weapons.

In addition to its sea and air defences, a military defence would require ground forces capable of repelling a limited attack which would also help to deter a full-scale attack. The regular army, with its mobile and armoured units, should be supplemented by larger numbers of reserves. Some territorial forces would be assigned to defend key installations, while others would play a harassing role until an invasion was repelled or the government surrendered.

In our view, there should be provision to continue resistance after a military defeat. This is the subject of the next chapter.

6. Strategies against Occupation

As things stand at the moment, neither Western Europe nor Britain would be occupied in the event of war – in all probability they would be destroyed. In considering non-nuclear defence, however, the risk of destruction is diminished, while occupation becomes a prospect to be taken more seriously.

A country in military conflict with a superpower is liable to have its conventional forces overwhelmed and to be forced to concede at least some territory. Moreover, in the nuclear age, any system of conventional military defence is vulnerable to the possibility of nuclear escalation or blackmail. Yet even though conventional forces may have to succumb to massive military might, resistance is still possible. Preparations for popular resistance could thus help to discourage a potential aggressor and, at worst, make it easier to wage a rearguard action to deny an occupier 'the fruits of victory'. This chapter therefore examines the types of resistance which could be mounted against a force of occupation or an attempt to install a client regime.

Strategies against occupation could be adopted as 'complementary' tactics to conventional defence, either providing additional means of harassment during the attack or, in the event of a successful invasion, being a 'fall-back' strategy. In principle, strategies against occupation could also be developed as a *substitute* for conventional preparations, as an approach to defence in its own right. Such a strategy would build on the existing and political and economic disincentives to attack.

There are enormous political and economic advantages for the Soviet Union in developing peaceful relations with Western Europe. But, if it tried to take over Western Europe by force, the Soviet Union would face daunting problems quite apart from the issue of military resistance. The complex industrial societies of Western Europe tend to be more prosperous and technologically more innovative than their Eastern bloc neighbours, their populations are accustomed to a higher material standard of living and many have long traditions of democratic organization. Whatever was the case in the late 1940s, the difficulties which would now beset the Soviet Union in trying to establish its style of government in West Germany would be enormous and would in their turn aggravate existing stresses in the East. Preparations for resistance would set out to reinforce these existing political and economic restraints. Thus, Soviet leaders, aware that there would be popular resistance to occupation, might hesitate to take on the problem of Poland several times over.

Any aggressor who expects that an occupation would meet determined resistance would think twice before embarking on an attack. A prolonged effort to impose their will on one country, let alone several, could place a severe strain on their machinery of domination – politically and economically, as well as militarily. By itself, awareness that a society was prepared to resist occupation might not dissuade an aggressor – especially if the object of the attack was short-term, such as the seizure of strategic facilities, rather than the lasting subjugation of a country. But in general it would enhance the dissuasive power of deterrence and defensive preparations to combat invasion.

The starting point for planning a strategy against occupation is the recognition that this is a struggle on uneven terms, a militarily mighty power confronting a much weaker country. Therefore, one needs to find forms of struggle which can render certain kinds of warfare much less effective or decisive. All strategy involves exploiting opponents' weaknesses and making the most of your own strengths. The main weakness of an occupation regime is that it depends to a large extent on the cooperation, or at least compliance, of the majority of the population. Conversely, the main strength of a resistance movement has to be popular morale – a widespread will to resist.

GUERRILLA WARFARE

Guerrilla warfare is in essence a protracted form of struggle, relying on a process of attrition to wear down enemy forces, on progressive demoralization to reduce their effectiveness and on a variety of political and economic pressures. Militarily, it seeks to catch the opponent off-guard with surprise tactics such as hit-and-run attacks and ambushes, never directly confronting a more powerful force but retreating, hiding and then attacking an enemy at their weakest points. By dispersing its forces, a guerrilla strategy aims at offering few military targets for heavy firepower.

Guerrilla tactics are designed more to weaken an opponent than to defend territory. While they could be used in harassing an invading force and delaying an attack, they are not suited to halting and repelling an invasion. Only in the final stages of a guerrilla war, when the opposing forces have been sufficiently depleted and one has accumulated the military strength to defeat them in regular warfare, would one engage in a set-piece battle. This pattern was seen in Vietnam, first leading up to the defeat of the French at Dien Bien Phu in 1954 and later in the 1960s and 1970s when guerrilla warfare culminated in essentially conventional offensives by the National Liberation Front in combination with the North Vietnamese army.

As a fall-back strategy in the event of invasion, guerrilla warfare could have a role in British defence in two contexts.

1. An underground military organization could operate along the lines of the 'secret armies' of northern Europe during the Second World War, coordinating its strategy with that of an outside power – effectively the US – which was still engaged in a military, non-nuclear campaign.

This scenario has parallels with the Second World War, but seems highly improbable in the present context. A prolonged war – where parts of Western Europe were under Soviet occupation but a large US force was still fighting for the liberation of Europe – would most likely escalate to a strategic nuclear exchange between the superpowers. Even if such a war remained non-nuclear, it would be so destructive that the countries on whose territories it was fought might choose to abandon regular warfare and rely on some form of protracted resistance.

For 'secret armies' to play a major role, outside military assistance could be critical. The experience of the Second World War indicates three respects in which this was so. First, the prospect of eventual liberation by an outside force played a vital part in sustaining the morale of the resistance. Second, resistance movements depended on Britain and other allies for the supply of arms and equipment and benefited from the trained personnel who were parachuted or smuggled into occupied Europe. Third, they were most effective militarily when their attacks were coordinated with allied strategy. Where uprisings took place prematurely, as in Naples in September 1943, or help from regular forces failed to arrive, as in Warsaw in August 1944, the result was a massacre.

While a secret army could perform a useful military function acting in concert with an outside conventional army, if there was no chance of being thus 'liberated', and if there was little military aid, the role of armed resistance movements would be limited. Although in the more peasant-based societies of southern and eastern Europe, Yugoslavia especially, partisans managed to build up sizeable forces, it would be unrealistic to expect similar achievements in highly urbanized, industrialized countries. Partisan forces operating from strongholds in the British countryside could hardly gather the power to challenge and defeat occupying forces in regular warfare, while an underground army using urban guerrilla tactics would be even less capable of transforming itself into a regular force capable of administering the final blow against an occupying power.

2. A more viable role for guerrilla resistance would be as one wing of a campaign of resistance involving other forms of disruption and civil unrest, putting political, economic and military pressure on the occupier to withdraw. Such a campaign could be conducted right across occupied Europe and would aim at the collapse of the occupation rather than at its defeat in battle.

The function of guerrilla warfare here would be to spark off, heighten and give a military edge to a more general struggle. In a situation where Soviet and Warsaw Pact forces were greatly overstretched trying to hold down the populations of Western Europe, and perhaps having to deal with rebellion in parts of Eastern Europe too, they could be forced to withdraw or make some compromises. This prospect would certainly enhance deterrence. Against such resistance, it would be hard to consolidate client regimes and there would be a strong possibility that this resistance would spill over, provoking crises in the Soviet Union's existing sphere of influence.

In this kind of strategy, however, guerrilla tactics would be very much a double-edged sword since the human and social costs of guerrilla warfare can be so extreme. First, a successful guerrilla raid is likely to provoke swingeing reprisals directed not against the guerrillas themselves but against the community at large. Not only is repression stepped up, but it tends to become more brutal, including torture, collective punishments against the communities thought to be harbouring the guerrillas and sometimes the wholesale revenge killing of unarmed civilians. In urban guerrilla warfare, where civilian dress is in effect a disguise enabling the guerrilla to melt back into the general population, civilians are particularly exposed.

Second, there is a perilously fine dividing line between guerrilla warfare and terrorism. Guerrilla warfare can be discriminate, aimed at the occupying armed forces or – more controversially – at aspects of their system of military/political control. Terrorism, on the other hand, does not distinguish between soldier and civilian and may be aimed at civilians of the same nationality as the occupying power or at civilians who do not openly oppose the occupying power. Placing bombs in pubs or shops, taking hostages at random in hijacks or in large-scale terrorization are morally intolerable, whatever their political efficacy. Urban guerrilla warfare especially is liable to degenerate into terrorism.

A third and fatefully long-term problem with guerrilla warfare as part of a mixed strategy of civil unrest is that it heightens social divisions. In the generalized climate of violence, and with weapons readily available, old scores may be settled and old feuds revived or new ones created between rival guerrilla groups. The killing of collaborators is common practice, despite the difficulty of judging where unavoidable cooperation ends and culpable collaboration begins. The enemy is no longer just the occupying power but increasingly someone's neighbour. The result is that, instead of cementing unity in opposition to an occupation, such guerrilla tactics leave deeply corrosive memories and conflicts far into the future.

Some guerrilla activity would be almost bound to occur spontaneously in the event of an occupation, but as a systematic strategy it could be unacceptably damaging. In our view, guerrilla warfare should not be included in planning the defence of Britain.

SABOTAGE

Sabotage can be a dramatic form of action, it can seriously hamper an occupier, and the threat of extensive sabotage may itself discourage invasion. Sabotage, however, is not in itself a strategy; it is more a set of tactics.

One could aim to slow down and hamper an invasion by sabotaging transport links – destroying bridges and tunnels, damaging airport runways, harbours, railway lines or motorways. This kind of action would certainly have a nuisance value and putting key facilities out of action could even deprive an occupier of the very assets the invasion was designed to gain – runways, for instance, or industrial plants which could be brought to a standstill simply by removing a crucial component. Announcing in advance that this is what one plans to do might give a potential invader pause. In the Second World War, Sweden and Switzerland's declarations that they would sabotage major communications and transport links certainly were a factor which helped to keep them out of the war.

While the more disruptive forms of sabotage are prominent in guerrilla warfare, less spectacular forms of sabotage, where the perpetrator could pass unnoticed, may suit a civil resistance campaign. Like other guerrilla tactics, dramatic sabotage raids run the risk of exposing the population to reprisals. These should, therefore, be rare events in a campaign of civil resistance, and carefully timed for maximum impact. But other, more unobtrusive types of sabotage are possible, from putting sand in petrol tanks or sugar in cement mixers to making deliberate mistakes when forced to work for the occupier. Computerization offers whole new areas of vulnerability to sneaky forms of sabotage.

An occupier, however, could live indefinitely with the kind of loss of efficiency achieved by sabotage. Sabotage needs to be combined with other elements of resistance into a strategy.

CIVIL RESISTANCE

Civil resistance is resistance by the civilian population in the form of strikes, boycotts, civil disobedience and mass non-cooperation. Its power springs from the fact that methods which have played a central role in economic and social struggles could be incorporated into a defence strategy, as occurred during the Second World War in German-occupied countries and in Czechoslovakia following the Soviet invasion in 1968.

States are largely dependent upon a measure of acquiescence from the majority of the population. As a defence policy, civil resistance would aim to deprive an occupation or puppet regime of its basis of social power while seeking to enlist support internationally, such as international sanctions against the aggressor and solidarity from at least some citizens of the aggressor state.

Unlike conventional warfare, civil resistance cannot physically halt or destroy invading forces. Unlike guerrilla warfare, it cannot deplete them by the cumulative effect of many small engagements. But it can plausibly aim to (a) make governing a country difficult if not impossible (as in thwarting attempted military takeovers such as the Kapp putsch of 1920 in Berlin and the Generals' Revolt in Algeria in 1961); (b) maintain the values, institutions and general culture of an occupied country; and (c) deny the opponent many of the political and economic benefits it might seek to gain from an occupation.

These are essentially defensive tasks. But the resistance must also aim to take the struggle into the opponent's camp, and so inflict costs in its turn. Thus it can aim to: (a) sow dissent and disaffection among the occupation forces (in Czechoslovakia, for instance, there is evidence that some of the troops were nonplussed by demonstrations and passive resistance during the 1968 invasion); (b) disrupt economic and cultural exchanges that existed between the countries before an attack (as when the Swiss threatened to blow up certain tunnels through the Alps in the event of a German invasion during the Second World War). In the East/West context, one would hope to show that there was more to be gained from continuing normal, peaceful trading relations than from any attempt to seize assets by force. Civil resistance also aims to: (c) mobilize international opinion against the attacker, for instance, through the United Nations and non-governmental bodies; and (d) work to bring about divisions, or widen existing divisions, within the opponent's forces and officials, and among leaders in the opponent's own country, culminating in undermining the opponent's authority at home.

What hope there is of achieving these aims would obviously depend on circumstances as well as upon the strategy adopted. In general, civil resistance could not be expected to achieve a quick victory against a foreign occupation. The occupied country is likely to divide into three groups: a small, strong-willed and highly motivated minority which would refuse allegiance to the conquerors; the majority which would accommodate itself to the situation, however unwillingly and resentfully; and a minority which would actively and treasonably collaborate. A strategy for civil resistance would have to take account of these divisions.

Such a strategy needs to envisage some distinct phases of struggle. As an initial phase, one possibility would be all-out defiance and non-cooperation – what has been called 'Non-violent Blitzkrieg'. An *indefinite* general strike is hardly a realistic response to invasion, and would probably end in a sense of demoralization and failure. But a deliberately short strike as part of a phase of intensive resistance could serve to mobilize the population for a longer-term struggle. This would be particularly appropriate if no military resistance had been offered, as it would provide dramatic evidence to the outside world that aggression had taken place and that the population was determined to oppose it.

Another possibility for the opening phase, especially following a military defeat, would put the emphasis on underground propaganda and symbolic acts of resistance. Here one would try to communicate with the opponent, primarily aiming at troops and functionaries as the leadership would probably be impervious to such appeals; with third parties (other governments and populations); and, most crucially, with one's own compatriots. Mobilizing the population and maintaining morale would be the key tasks, taking care not to offer the new rulers a pretext for further repression.

The initial phase could be followed by a period of *selective resistance*, focused on areas or objectives of special importance in the struggle. This might involve defending institutions and freedoms which are central to the indigenous culture, or seeking to deny some of the attacker's major objectives. The resistance of Norwegian teachers to the introduction of a Nazi-style curriculum in the schools and to the establishment of a state-controlled union was a fine example of this. One advantage of selective resistance is that it is able to shift the burden of responsibility from one section of the community to another, rather than calling upon the whole society all at once in a campaign of total defiance which it would be difficult to sustain. In this phase, all-out resistance would be appropriate on occasions as a response to severe brutalities or to support particular groups under attack.

Passive and 'semi'-resistance is also likely to be important during this phase, especially in the face of ruthless repression. This can involve go-slows, economic and administrative obstruction, 'Schweikism' (after the irrepressibly incompetent *Good Soldier Schweik*) and the kind of general bloody-mindedness that characterized the popular response to occupation in Europe and which is a common feature of everyday resistance to unreasonable demands from on high. The great advantage of semi-resistance is that it is difficult to detect and may therefore be carried out with relative impunity, enabling one to frustrate even the most dictatorial regime. More open forms of indirect resistance could also be appropriate, such as wearing badges, singing resistance songs, observing days of national mourning or celebration – visible expressions of resistance which are not so challenging as to bring down on the population the full repressive wrath of the regime.

A campaign which combines this kind of passive and semi-resistance on the one hand, with periodic climaxes involving mass open defiance on the other, could probably be sustained over a long period. Resistance would not be confined to the activist minority, but would involve the less committed majority in less conspicuous and lower-risk forms of resistance. In Denmark during the German occupation there were two major 'battles' – the rescue of 95 per cent of Danish Jews by spiriting them away to Sweden in October 1943, and the nine-day general strike in Copenhagen in July 1944. The backdrop to this, however, was a continuous low-key resistance, taking the form of 'civil conscious-ness' programmes, mass patriotic sing-songs and the kind of 'they-can't-touch-you-for-it' obstructiveness where a German mine-sweeper took twenty-six months to be built, instead of the usual nine months, and in the end never did go into service because of successive acts of sabotage.

The last phase of the resistance aims finally to dislodge the occupation or client regime. When the opponent is weakened, perhaps when discontent is rife in the occupying force, and when the population has built up its strength and confidence, an all-out drive to achieve liberation could once again be launched – a phase of open and large-scale resistance.

Historically, campaigns of civil resistance against occupations have usually been improvised, often arising in circumstances where armed resistance would have been suicidal. Yet there have been successes. During the early period of the Second World War, when Hitler's armies seemed invincible, civil resistance – often in the forms of strikes – was used to obstruct his policies, most notably with the Norwegian teachers' strike but also in the Netherlands.

In evaluating the achievements of civil resistance, it is essential to compare them with the likely consequences of other methods. In 1956, Imry Nagy and other leaders were executed following the Hungarian uprising. In Czechoslovakia in 1968, on the other hand, the popular non-violent resistance forced the Soviet Union into a remarkable climb-down, releasing the arrested leaders and negotiating a settlement which kept Dubcek in power until April 1969. The resistance failed to halt the invasion and the terms of the Moscow Accords signed by Dubcek and Svoboda enabled the Soviet Union to rescind the liberalizing reforms and to carry out a massive purge. However, the failure did not so much lie in the non-violent methods as in the reliance on a political leadership which – kept in isolation in Moscow – did not appreciate the scope and potential of the resistance; once the Accords had been signed, further resistance was virtually paralysed.

In spite of this outcome, one achievement of the Czechoslovakian resistance may have been to increase the dissuasive power of popular resistance by showing the Soviet Union that it is dangerous to expose troops to the arguments and appeals of unarmed civilians. Some Soviet troops were so bewildered that their 'friendly intervention' was rejected not by 'counter-revolutionaries' but by the people at large, that they had to be replaced by fresh troops who would obey orders more reliably. The Soviet Union will not lightly risk putting its troops in a situation which, by its very nature, will pose questions about their duty, provoking, if not mutiny, at least perplexed discontent.

A lesson for any future resistance movement is to protect political leaders as far as possible from the pressures to make unnecessary concessions. Advance plans should provide for a government-in-exile which would be charged with the task of negotiating with the invader. Its prime function would be to undercut any attempt to bestow legitimacy on a client regime and so to mobilize international support for the resistance. In the case of Britain, a government-in-exile might be based in a Commonwealth country willing to accept political refugees and to provide broadcasting facilities.

There are other ways, too, in which preparation could make resistance more effective. Not least, publicizing the existence, if not the details, of such preparations would serve as a warning to a potential invader. In Britain, the organizational base for civil resistance would probably be existing political, trade union, cultural and religious bodies. As civil resistance is an inherently decentralized form of struggle, it would be vital that the initiative should reside less with a central body than with the network of local organizations. These could be brought together in a coordinating committee for civil resistance similar to the body set up in Norway at the beginning of the German occupation, but with national committees for Wales, Scotland, Northern Ireland and England.

In peacetime, this committee would try to ensure that the hardware for civil resistance would be available – that is, means of publishing, broadcasting, communicating and coordination. But attention to the software is even more important. At the moment, despite the experience of trade unions and other sections of the population, there is considerable scepticism about the potential of civil resistance. The committee would therefore have an important educational role, making a hard-headed assessment of what it could hope to achieve through civil resistance and outlining the form such a campaign might take and the variety of activities it might include.

There is a growing body of research on civil resistance as a means of defence and several governments have commissioned research projects on the subject. As well as arousing the interest of some church bodies and political parties such as the German Greens, civil resistance has found advocates among the military – most notably, Sir Stephen King-Hall and Basil Liddell Hart in Britain and General de Bollardière in France. Unfortunately, there has been little official interest in this in Britain. A non-nuclear government should seek to rectify this neglect, funding research with a view to the eventual formation of a committee to plan for civil resistance. Official support would help not only in providing funds, but also as a way of indicating the importance of this form of defence.

CONCLUSIONS

Strategies against occupation in general involve a prolonged struggle and are hardly relevant to the seizure of strategic outposts and outlying areas. They can be of vital importance, however, in frustrating an attempt to subjugate a whole society. While the Commission concluded that Britain and Western Europe are not well suited to guerrilla warfare, we agreed that civil resistance potentially has a significant contribution to make to a non-nuclear defence strategy.

While a minority of the Commission favoured a system of

77

exclusively non-violent defence, most of the Commission concluded that a military capability was essential to defence and that, for the foreseeable future, this would remain the predominant element. If a non-nuclear military defence is adopted, however, it would be important to hold non-violent resistance as a fall-back strategy to meet certain kinds of threats, such as nuclear blackmail. As a fall-back strategy, civil resistance would enhance dissuasion against aggression and would offer the best hope for resisting occupation.

Summary of Recommendations

A nuclear-disarmed Britain should not accept NATO's current nuclear-based strategy. Britain could, however, seek to initiate a process of nuclear disarmament in Europe by staying in the alliance on the condition that NATO moves decisively towards abandoning any reliance on a nuclear strategy. This would imply NATO taking the following steps:

1. Withdrawing Pershing II and cruise missiles
2. Declaring a policy of no-first-use of nuclear weapons
3. Withdrawing short-range, 'battlefield' nuclear weapons
4. Withdrawing 'theatre' nuclear weapons
5. Ending reliance on US nuclear weapons as an element of its strategy.

As part of this process, NATO would obviously seek reciprocal measures of disarmament by the Soviet Union. But the commitment to de-nuclearize NATO should be unconditional and would therefore not depend on Soviet reciprocation.

Most members of the Commission favoured this approach, arguing that if NATO did not decisively shift away from its nuclear strategy within the lifetime of one British government, Britain should withdraw from the alliance. It could then explore the possibility of alternative approaches to the collective security in Europe, or adopt a non-aligned position.

Most members of the Commission also wanted Britain and Western Europe to retain a sizeable conventional military deterrent at least in the short to medium term, or pending negotiated arms reductions, but argued that this should be an unmistakably defensive posture. This would mean having the capacity to inflict heavy losses on any invading force, but at most only a limited capacity to mount offensive operations in the opponent's territory. Renouncing nuclear weapons would be a major step in this direction; it could be extended by, for instance, limiting the number of tanks, eliminating long-range bombers and emphasizing the role of part-time territorial soldiers.

A fall-back strategy of primarily non-violent, civil resistance should be adopted to meet the possible contingency of nuclear escalation or blackmail, or in the event of military defeat and occupation.

The focus of this book has been on the defence alternatives to nuclear strategy. Equally important, however, are the political opportunities which would arise from renouncing nuclear weapons. Our forthcoming follow-up report on the politics of alternative defence seeks to redefine British foreign policy and security goals. It looks at the chances for better relations in Europe which have foundered on the polarization into two rigid military blocs, examines the conditions for a stable peace in Europe and makes proposals to heal the divisions of Europe. Finally, beyond Europe, it takes stock of some of the urgent problems of a world in crisis and asks what Britain, Western Europe and movements for peace and justice can do.

Appendices

A: THE BALANCE OF CONVENTIONAL FORCES IN EUROPE

There is no wholly satisfactory method of estimating the military balance between the conventional forces of NATO and the Warsaw Pact.[1]

Comparing total numbers of troops does not account for the many NATO and Soviet commitments outside the 'central front'. Comparing forces deployed in, or near, the central front region, as the British government does in presenting its annual statement on the Defence Estimates, has greater validity but this too has shortcomings. First, it does not indicate the level or quality of reinforcements available to either side, nor the speed with which they could be transported to the central front. Second, it does not consider the reliability, efficiency and morale of a particular country's armed forces. Third, static assessments of this nature do not indicate the interactions between weapons systems in conflict, tanks versus anti-tank weapons for instance. Finally, it is not possible to specify the various levels of attack likely.

Table 2: *The British Government's View of the Balance of Forces on the Central Front*

	NATO	Ratio	Warsaw Pact
Total soldiers	800,000	1:1.2	980,000
Soldiers in fighting units	590,000	1:1.2	740,000
Main battle tanks	7,800	1:2.3	18,000
Artillery	3,000	1:2.7	8,200
Anti-tank guided			
weapons (inc. helicopters)	7,900	1:1.3	10,300
Fixed-wing tactical aircraft	1,300	1:2.1	2,700

In response to some of these problems, the US Department of Defense has developed the system of Armoured Division Equivalents (ADEs). This system assesses the mobility, firepower and survivability of all weaponry in every division on the central front to derive an estimate of the ADEs.[2] Although the exact number of ADEs is classified, the ratio is not – **for standing forces on the central front this is 1.2:1 in favour of the Warsaw Pact.**

Conclusions. Most assessments of the conventional balance inflate the Warsaw Pact advantage. To counter the Warsaw Pact's numerical advantages, the West has relied on its technological lead which, although much shorter now, still remains. Given the advantages of the defence in war, the Warsaw Pact does not have the kind of superiority necessary for a successful invasion of Western Europe. As the International Institute for Strategic Studies has maintained for many years: 'the conventional overall balance is such as to make general military aggression a highly risky undertaking. Though tactical redeployment could certainly provide a local advantage in numbers sufficient to allow an attacker to believe that he might achieve limited tactical success in some exposed areas, there would still appear to be insufficient overall strength on either side to guarantee victory.'[3]

Notes

1. For an overview of the problems of assessing the military balance, see A. Kelly, 'Not by Numbers Alone: Assessing the Military Balance', *Peace Studies Paper No. 11*, University of Bradford/Housmans, London, 1984.

2. See J. Mearsheimer, *Conventional Deterrence*, Cornell University Press, 1983.

3. *The Military Balance, 1984–85*, IISS, London, 1984, p.151.

B: POSSIBLE FORCE STRUCTURES FOR AN INDEPENDENT BRITISH DEFENCE POLICY

Here we present three possible force structures for a non-nuclear Britain pursuing an independent defence policy. These all start from Britain's present military strength; they all assume that Britain would move towards abandonment of its global role; and

they all represent possible interpretations of a 'high entry price' policy.

Structure 1 represents a Swedish-style force structure, taking into account that Britain's land-mass is smaller but its population much larger and that a purely professional army should be more efficient than a largely conscript army.

Structure 2 lays less stress on ground forces, while maintaining a significant sea and air defence. Both Structures 1 and 2 posit a stronger air defence and maritime air support than the present forces allocated specifically to the defence of Britain itself.

Structure 3 sets lower levels for the army and for air defence and reduces the number of large vessels in favour of more patrol craft.

These are targets, assuming a five-year period of adjustment for the army, ten for the airforce and twenty for the navy.

Table 3: *Possible Force Structures for a Non-nuclear Britain*

ARMY (by year 5)[1]			
	Structure 1	Structure 2	Structure 3
Regular army	160,000	80,000	50,000
Ready reserves	350,000	70,000	70,000

AIRFORCE (by Year 10)		
	Structures 1 and 2	Structure 3
Personnel	60,000	48,000
Aircraft (front-line units)[2]		
strike/attack	0	0
ground support	48 (Harriers)	48
maritime patrol	28	28
reconnaissance	36 (Jaguars)	24
air defence	112	64
airborne early warning	11	11
maritime support	48 (strike)	24 (strike)
	36 (air cover)	24 (air cover)
Total (combat and reconnaissance)	319	223

AIRFORCE (by Year 10) *continued*

	Structures 1 and 2	Structure 3
Air transport		
fixed-wing	0	0
helicopters	54	54
Tanker	0	0
Search and rescue	16	16
Total	389	293
Surface-to-air missiles	12 squadrons	6 squadrons

NAVY

	Structures 1 and 2			Structure 3	
	Year 1	Year 10	Year 20	Year 10	Year 20
Personnel			35,000		28,000
Vessels					
ASW carriers	3	0	0	0	0
submarines	27	16	16	16	16
destroyers	12	8	0	6	0
frigates	44	24	21	24	12
patrol craft					
(large)	12	20	26	25	40
mine-sweepers/					
hunters	34	36	38	36	38

Notes

1. These projections assume consistency of defence planning from Year 1 of a non-nuclear Britain to Year 20.

2. There would be additional training, communications and liaison light aircraft.

C: MEMBERS OF THE ALTERNATIVE DEFENCE COMMISSION (JANUARY 1985)

Paddy Ashdown, MP, Liberal Member for Yeovil

Viv Bingham, President of the Liberal Party, 1981–2

April Carter, writer and lecturer; former Politics Tutor, Somerville College, Oxford

Owen Greene, Researcher on nuclear weapons issues at the Open

University; author of *Europe's Folly: The Facts and Arguments about Cruise* (1983)

Malcolm Harper, Director, United Nations Association

Mary Kaldor, Science Policy Research Unit, University of Sussex; author of *The Baroque Arsenal* (1982)

Isobel Lindsay, Member of the National Executive of the Scottish National Party; Lecturer in Sociology at Strathclyde University

Terry Moran, Lucas Aerospace Combine Shop Stewards Committee

James O'Connell, Professor of Peace Studies, University of Bradford

Rev. Paul Oestreicher, British Council of Churches; member of the Church of England Working Party which produced the report, *The Church and the Bomb* (1982)

Michael Randle, Research Fellow, University of Bradford; Co-ordinator

Paul Rogers, Senior Lecturer in Peace Studies, University of Bradford; Chair

Elizabeth Sigmund, Co-ordinator of the Working Party on Chemical and Biological Weapons; author of *Rage Against the Dying* (1980)

Dan Smith, independent research worker on UK defence policy; author of *The Defence of the Realm in the 1980s* (1980)

Jonathan Steele, Chief Foreign Correspondent of the *Guardian*; author of *World Power: Soviet Foreign Policy Under Brezhnev and Andropov* (1983)

Walter Stein, former Senior Lecturer in Literature and Philosophy, Department of Adult Education and Extra Mural Studies, University of Leeds; editor of *Nuclear Weapons and Christian Conscience* (1961; 1981)

Dafydd Elis Thomas, MP, Plaid Cymru Member for Meirionnydd

Ron Todd, General Secretary Elect, Transport and General Workers' Union

Andrew Wilson, Associate Editor and former Defence Correspondent of the *Observer*; author of *The Disarmer's Handbook* (1983)

Commission Researchers: Howard Clark, Lisa Foley

D: PUBLICATIONS BY THE ALTERNATIVE DEFENCE COMMISSION
Defence Without the Bomb, Taylor and Francis (312pp., £4.45)
'Non-Nuclear Defence and Civil Nuclear Power', Supplementary Paper No. 1 (16pp., 60p)
'Domestic Political Implications of Non-Nuclear Defence', Supplementary Paper No. 2 (16pp., 60p)
'Economic Defence' (Safeguards Against Economic Threats), Supplementary Paper No. 3 (16pp., 60p)
'Threat or Opportunity: The Economic Consequences of Non-Nuclear Defence', Supplementary Paper No. 4 and Peace Research Report No. 6 (68pp., £1.25)

All the above publications are available from Housmans, 5 Caledonian Road, London N1, and the School of Peace Studies, University of Bradford, Bradford, West Yorkshire, BD7 1DP.

Notes

Chapter 1

1. 'Economic Defence', Alternative Defence Commission Supplementary Paper No. 3 (see Appendix D.)

Chapter 4

1. These possibilities will be discussed in our second report.

2. Dale R. Herspring and Ivan Volgyes, 'How Reliable are East European Armies', *Survival*, September/October 1980, XXIL(5), pp. 208–18.

3. US Army Training and Doctrine Command (TRADOC) Pamphlet 525–5, *US Army Operational Concepts: The AirLand Battle and Corps 86*, 25 March 1981, p. 12.

4. 'Soviet Operational Concepts in the 1980s', *Strengthening Conventional Deterrence*, ESECS, Macmillan, 1983, pp. 105–36.

5. The US and Britain are considering the deployment of conventionally-armed Minuteman missiles in Britain, targeted on Warsaw Pact airfields – *Aviation Week and Space Technology*, 9 July 1984.

6. F. Barnaby and S. Windass, 'Non-Provocative Defence', *Briefing Paper No. 2*, Just Defence (The Rookery, Adderbury, Banbury, Oxon., 1983). See also F. Barnaby and E. Boeker, 'Defence Without Offence', *Peace Studies Paper No. 8*, University of Bradford/Housmans, 1982.

7. See Horst Afheldt, 'Tactical Nuclear Weapons and European Security' in Stockholm International Peace Research Institute, *Tactical Nuclear Weapons: European Perspectives*, Taylor and Francis, 1978, pp. 262–95.

Index